YoungWriters

Past Voices - Future Voices

2010 Poetry Competition for 11-18 year-olds

Middlesex & Surrey

Edited by Mark Richardson

First published in Great Britain in 2010 by

YoungWriters

Remus House
Coltsfoot Drive
Peterborough
PE2 9JX
Telephone: 01733 890066
Website: www.youngwriters.co.uk

Book Design by Ali Smith & Tim Christian

SB ISBN 978-0-85739-032-5

Foreword

Young Writers was established in order to promote creativity and a love of reading and writing in children and young adults. We believe that by offering them a chance to see their own work in print, their confidence will grow and they will be encouraged to become the poets of tomorrow.

Our latest competition 'Past Poets - Future Voices' was specifically designed as a showcase for secondary school pupils, giving them a platform with which to express their ideas, aspirations and passions. In order to expand their skills, entrants were encouraged to use different forms, styles and techniques.

Selecting the poems for publication was a difficult yet rewarding task and we are proud to present the resulting anthology. We hope you agree that this collection is an excellent insight into the voices of the future.

Contents

St Paul's Catholic College, Sunbury-on-Thames

Stowford College, Sutton

The Green School, Isleworth

The Matthew Arnold School, Staines

The Royal Ballet School, Richmond

The Tiffin Girls' School, Kingston-upon-Thames

Tiffin School, Kingston-upon-Thames

Tolworth Girls' School, Surbiton

The Poems

Do I Look Unusual?

Do you count me any different because of my scarf?
My scarf is my protection: it's My own decision
I am *not* under any oppression.

I sometimes think you're very sad,
From time to time you lose control, are you under a lot of pressure?
You feel you have to follow the fashion,
What's your motivation? Have a little imagination!

For you it all seems such a burden,
Why don't you think open-mindedly, and explain your objection?
I have a book that I follow, a book that tells me how to dress,
It's not a magazine, no, no, no, but something else . . . can you guess?

It is the Qur'an, the blessed book,
Sent to the Muslims by Almighty God,
Who revealed it to our Blessed Prophet
Muhammad (peace and blessings be upon him) who is our guide.

Do I make fun of the way *you* dress?
Even though sometimes you look a mess,
Covered in tattoos from head to toe,
Sometimes hardly wearing any clothes.
But that's *your* choice, just as I have mine, isn't this a democratic society?

Sometimes I wish I could really tell you,
A few little things I'd like to share with you,
But somehow I seem to always hold back,
I hold back not because I'm scared, *no,* fear not,
It's because I want you to have a good impression
Of my faith and of different people.

Let's try to have a little understanding of each other and remember . . .
We are all descendants of Prophet Adam, all part of one big family,
So let's try to learn from one another,
And show some respect for each other.

Now the time has come to end, I'm glad we got to have this chat.
I sincerely wish you all the very best,
May God shower His blessings upon us *all!*

Imaan Qureshy (13)

Humanity

What right, does a human own,
To reserve a hatred for all knowledge unknown?
To believe they rule, Mother Nature's world,
To deconstruct DNA, double helixs uncurled,
To mess with creations, they can't call their own,
But when something falters, the consequences will be shown.
We need to see the big picture, and see that it needs change
For the benefit of the future, our ignorance is strange,
We humans are not leaders, for all we do is wrong,
Deforestation, CO_2 are factors of irrelevance, for she won't live long,
We are killing her off, slaughtering her work.
She deserves this not, her soul is locked,
Into the very fabric of this Earth,
For it is to us she gave birth.
To create a disease, is pretty darn low,
To inflict pain on life, is inhumane you know -
Why is our goal to destroy what we can,
To dig for diamonds, gold and rubies, jewels for Man?
We are heating up the world, through all means possible,
Combustion engines to oil rigs extracting tonnes of crude oil,
We put our social lives before our environment, that isn't good,
Because our planet should come first and we all know it should,
We are selfish and ignorant, the fact is we don't care,
About our children's generation, our meaningless traits they will share,
As to modify a machine, is correct and it's useful,
But to modify an animal, is just plain evil.
There's no justification that will back up that act,
For we borrow this world and should leave it intact.

Glenn Nigel Roberts (15)

A Quick Move

Hot scorching heat had me screaming
The rush, hurry and things made me worry
I ran upstairs and grabbed my bag,
Jumped into the bus and felt so mad.

The bus moved off, speeding down the road,
The house was out of sight! But *not* out of mind!

My face went pale and made me sad
I wondered if I would ever see it again,
My house in the desert, my school and my friends,
This is where I belong, I felt anger and pain.

The adventures we had going out and about,
Days out at the pool, splashing about,
Visiting the farm and playing in the well,
Things would never be the same again.

The airport came into sight
I wanted to scream with all my might!

Where I lived would never be the same
But I wasn't sure until I came
But when I came it wasn't bad
But still inside I still feel so sad

So this is where we are for now,
But who knows what the future will bring,
Adventures in Africa, China or back to Tarim!
But still inside I want to leave
And now and then I still feel sad
But I am OK now . . . so don't feel bad!

Khadijah Qureshy (11)

How To Live A Healthy Life

If you know what's good for you,
You'll listen to me now,
Just give up all the bad things
And I'll tell you what and how.

Think about your body,
What is junk food doing to you?
Do you feel tired and weary
Or as fit as a kangaroo?

If you eat fruit and vegetables,
Even the ones with a seed,
You'll have so much relentless energy
You could be a cheetah with rapid speed.

You need to burn off all those calories,
To do that you need to walk and run,
You need to do a lot of exercise
Whether it's fog, rain or sun.

If you don't do these things,
Your life will be like grains of sand,
Blown away from your life,
And your beauteous land.

If you do all these things,
I can guarantee,
You'll be fit and healthy,
And maybe live until ninety-three!

Tammy Samuel (13)

Reflection

He stares right into my eyes.
His eyes are full of hatred,
Full of anger and madness.
But yet he is just a boy.

As our eyes remain stagnant,
His eyes start to disclose a truth.
His anger starts to fade.
But yet he is just a boy.

Beyond the anger,
Is despair,
Misery and desperation.
Yet he is just a boy.

All he wants
Is to be heard,
To be loved.
Yet he is just a boy.

I see that boy often,
In the same place
Day and night,
It's what I see in the mirror.

Benjamin Grant (15)

Forest

The wind blows sharply through the trees,
And the mountains behind start roaring.
More softly than falling peas,
The rain starts pouring.

Campers run into their tent,
Hiding from the rain.
More time there they have spent,
Than eating down by the lane.

Small animals tiptoe across,
Trying not to make a sound.
Jumping over scattered moss,
Treading carefully on the ground.

Scattered leaves crunch
As the campers have their brunch
They're autumn-brown
And all around
In the forest.

Maaria Hanif (12)

Loneliness

I can't be on my own,
I hate to be alone.
The silence swallows me whole
Like being stuck in a black hole.

The darkness is the worst
Like a cold creeping curse.
Loneliness creeps in, fear knocks on the door.
The sadness sails in like a boat into a harbour.

The truth leaks out like ink from a pen,
Carefully crashing, creating chaos then . . .
A chill scratches through your body
But there is nobody.

Isolation is a path many are travelling,
Tears are silently splashing,
Fear is a downward passage leading nowhere:
It isn't fun and it's not fair.

Katie Banks (13)

Friendship

What are friends?
Friends are people that you can trust and someone that will help you,
Friends are people that you can talk about your problems to and cheer you up,
Friends are people, who you can have a laugh with and play with,
Friends are there for you when you are feeling sad or lonely,
Friends are there to comfort you,
Friends are people that you should keep close to you,
Friends are people that support you through good times and bad times,
Friends are people that you can have fun with,
Friends are people that you can joke with and play pranks on
But most importantly, friends will be there forever.

Emily Jane Murphy (13)
Collingwood College, Camberley

Life's A Roller Coaster

I watch as the roller coaster twists and turns,
Gallops up and down,
Flips over and under,
Gaining energy as it climbs, then releasing it as it falls.
Through the rain and sunshine,
In the dark and light.
It makes some people scream and shout,
Others smile and laugh,
Its audience of all ages include children and adults.

Ecstatic excitement,
Thrill,
Anxiety,
Fear,
Laughter,
Screams,
Rattles, thunder . . . then silence.

But no - no silence.
My head is still buzzing.
So many thoughts flouting each other,
Voices I want to voice,
Dreams I wish to pursue,
People I want to meet,
The life I want to live.

I don't want to waste time dreaming,
I am determined to break free,
Away from the inner world and into the exterior
Onto the roller coaster.
The real life.
I am approaching.
I will do it.
I believe . . .
I will definitely do it.

I will climb . . .
I will fall . . .
But I will certainly do it!

Shanie Khalid (18)
Collingwood College, Camberley

National Poetry Competition

I may not be the best
But I don't think I'm the worst
Jumping jumps at 3ft 6
On my trusty horse Brownie
We have an unbreakable bond

Entering competitions
Hoping to win a trophy
Or maybe even a rosette
Anything is possible
If you're lucky you could get both

Dressage is OK
Show jumping I'm good at
But I love cross country
Eventing is my passion
Horse riding is my dream

When I ride it's like another world
Jumping is like I'm high in the heavens
I love my horse
He is my everything
Even though he is bad-mannered

Horse riding is my life
I hope to be a famous rider one day
Maybe even ride at Olympia
Or maybe Hickstead

I see my horse every day
Even when the sky is grey
I give him lots of treats
But only when he's good

Brownie is the best and I love him to bits
I have no idea what I would do without him.

Bryony Muir
Collingwood College, Camberley

The Shelby Mustang

Sleek and stylish, a work of art
Revving the engine, ready to start
Rear wheel drive, a 2-seat coupe
You don't want to get in this thing's way.
6 speed gearbox, supercharged V8
0 to 60 in 3.8
Quarter of a mill, is a lot of beans
But not for one of these mean machines
Under the bonnet is an animal waiting to be unleashed
My interest in this car never fails to cease

A sculpted body, a real looker
A beautiful paint job, really pukka
Headlights that pierce the night into submission
Shame that this thing weighs more than a ton
This monstrous beast can't wait for the tarmac
It's a scythe of madness ready to hack
A high performance GT
Especially with 540 BHP
Aerodynamic, better handling
It's high up in quality ratings

A super car, muscle car, it's fantastic
The latest in a long line of American classics
As you approach this car your knees will be shaking
Because it has such a high horse power rating
Better handling and high-speed stability
Doesn't make this car soft and prissy
A modern look, the interior boasts
Just right for cruising along by the coast
After 45 years in production
The Mustang still looks hungrily at the world.

David Cook (12)
Collingwood College, Camberley

Homework

Homework is useless
We shouldn't have to do it
We do enough at school
So I say bye-bye to it

I hate homework
But there isn't any debate
We will always have homework
And work quite late

I really hate homework
I don't see the point
It can be too long
And all the writing hurts my wrist joint

I always give in my homework
Because if I don't the teachers will mention
That I'll be back after school
For a detention

I hate homework
I got too distracted
With brothers and sisters running around
I get sidetracked

I hate homework
It is boring
We do enough at school
And homework's just not cool

So we've come to a conclusion
That we shouldn't have to do it
So like I said
Bye-bye to it.

James Beere (13)
Collingwood College, Camberley

Football

You kick
You watch
You play
You score
You punt
You start
You pass
You receive
You cross
You celebrate
You cheer
You learn
You pass
You throw
You chant
You skip
You dodge
You shoot
You dance
You joke
You grow
You reach
You whack
You jeer
You think
You laugh
You cry
You jump
You hit
You dream!

Lewis Holliday (13)
Collingwood College, Camberley

My Pets

When I feel alone, down or upset,
There is nothing I love more than being with my pets,
My dog is tender, loving and caring,
Quiet, gentle, light-hearted and sharing,
He doesn't say a word but I know what he says,
For animals speak to us in different ways.

My cat may hiss, scratch and bite,
She may often wind up in a fight,
But somewhere inside her, this I know,
Is a sweet little kitty, wanting to show,
Her affection for me, for everyone,
Really all she wants is to have fun.

My little kitten is a different matter,
Around her is constant bangs and clatter,
Destruction always left in her wake,
There is no limit to the mess she can make,
But still she has time in her busy schedule,
To chill, relax and retain her cool.

The fish don't do much but swim and glug,
It's not as if you can give them hugs,
But for me they do fascinate with twists and twirls,
Elegant movements, tails in curls,
Their antics never do cease to amaze,
Me and my always wondrous gaze.

So with love unconditional and friendship forever,
Will this love ever end? No . . . never.

Catrina Sykes (13)
Collingwood College, Camberley

The Most Unusual Thing I've Ever Leapt From?

Dramatic monologue in Duffy's style (inspired by *Stealing*)

The most unusual thing I've ever leapt from?
A phonebox. Midday. It looked magnificent; a tall silver box to leap from.
I wanted the thrill of the adrenaline as I leapt from it.
I started to climb.

Better off dead than not doing what you want.
It was higher than I expected, a powerful fear piercing my gut.
Part of the thrill was knowing people were watching me.
How arrogant.

Sometimes I climb things with no purpose. Sprint up a wall for no reason,
Climb a building just to have a look.
I watch my bare hand scrabble up a wall, a strange roof.
Gravel. I let out a breath of air - Argh.

It took some time to learn all of this. I wasn't the same anymore.
I took a run and flew from the roof.
Again. Again. My breath ripped out in rags. It seems daft now.
Then I was standing alone reprimanded by Miss Hanif.
Sick of her.

Boredom. Mostly I'm so bored I could climb the Eiffel Tower.
One time, I climbed a pub because I saw more to climb and leap from.
I saw a gap between two garages once, I made it mine.
But the phonebox was the strangest.
You have absolutely no idea what I'm saying, do you?

Peter Breakspear (15)
Collingwood College, Camberley

Log Fire

My log fire stays at the side of the room,
The faces carved,
Look down and listen to our stories told.

As the struck match, nears the flaky wood,
A light glistens the room,
Catching the attention of the family around.

Not one spot of darkness, covers the room,
The family sits round,
The flames reach out towards them.

The heat like the sun,
Makes faces red and hands blue no more,
The happiness can be seen.

From the young to the elderly, all is well
With everyone wrapped up,
To keep out the cold.

Even though it is winter and a chill is outside,
No one in the room is moaning,
'Cause they've got their log fire lit.

As the night goes on though, with the family curled up,
The spitting of the fire shortly stops,
Till nothing remains but the hot, burnt ash.

Even though the heat has vanished in the room,
The faces carved still stare,
From the log fire wall.

Christopher Walsh (13)
Collingwood College, Camberley

Running

The gunshot went, feet were rushing
People cheering all around us.
Jostling for position at the front of the pack
Waiting for the first corner to arrive.
We headed off into the dark eerie woods,
The hardest part of the daring course.
There were roots shooting up all around,
People dodging, weaving, falling and jumping.
Myself and two others made it through to the clearing
With not a moment to spare!
We turned the tight corner, three of us in a group all close together,
So close we could feel each other's breath.
Then I saw it, I saw the tape.
I started to sprint,
But with every stride I took
It felt like the line was getting further and further away.
Then suddenly I was there, one stride away.
I broke the tape and looked across.
I was clear.
I had won.
Everything became real again, now I could hear everything.
The roar of the crowd, the rush of footsteps rushing to congratulate me.
My brother took me in his arms.
I took a deep breath, I had done it!

Steve Payne (12)
Collingwood College, Camberley

The Runaway

When I left a tear fell from my eye.

As I walked away, all I could hear in my head was,
I hate my life, I hate it.
I was so envious of all of them,
How their smiles glistened like a moonlit sky.

How they were loved and I was not.

I had a life, a shameful life.
I had friends, family
I did not deserve.

I had love, but it tore me apart every time.
Hate, that knew me too well.

People called me names, taunted me,
I couldn't bear it anymore.

I ran, only a few feet,
Then I heard a scream of horror,
As my mother read the letter.

Should I turn back now,
Stop all this grief

No!

Is what I have done right,
What you have done?

Alice Houghton (13)
Collingwood College, Camberley

The River

The river, I wish it were clear,
I wish I could see the fish,
With their bright scales gleaming in the sun but
No!
Dark green.
Dark blue.
Dark brown.
But still the hot sun beats down,
It makes the river shimmer and shine.

Quiet, almost silent.
Noise by the river,
A green grass snake
Slowly, silently slithering.
The green strings of the grass,
Bending slowly under the weight of the snake.
Its tongue moving in and out in time to my heartbeat.

Screams fill the air,
The ground rattles and shakes,
Children stampeding towards the river,
Yellows, reds, blues running without a care,
Splash splashing laughter everywhere.

Day filled with colours, sounds and laughter,
My day by the river.

Aidan West (16)
Collingwood College, Camberley

Poem

Have I told you how much I love you?
Your beautiful eyes light up the sky,
In our world just you and me,
Is our passion and love that could never be,
I try to keep strong through tough times,
But whatever happens we will glide,
Our future could be so bright,
With the beam of your light,
Your eyes, lips and soul,
Make me so whole,
With your beautiful heart,
It's like a love dart,
Our memories are so strong,
When we were so young,
I knew you were the one,
Nothing could ever tear us apart,
Except if you broke my heart,
I've never thought I would know someone as sweet as you,
And then I knew it was true when I saw you,
To me from you I thought we were glued,
For ever and ever I loved you,
I didn't really know what love was before I met you,
Till the first day I saw you.

Nicole Clift (13)
Collingwood College, Camberley

It Is . . .

It is something to do
I do it every day
It brings me joy, it keeps me entertained
You can do nearly anything on it
It is something to keep me relaxed when I'm stressed
It was worth buying one
It's like a super sun
It burns my time when days are long
The whole family can enjoy
Not just one lonely boy
It puts me in my happy place
You can even see it on my face
What do you think I'm talking about?
My Xbox
It brings a world of imagination
Along with it
It has made my life
So full of joy
I'm so grateful
The day I got it
It was the best day of my life
Now every day is.

Scott McCartney (12)
Collingwood College, Camberley

The Normal Day

When I wake up,
I wish I could just stay there,
And lie in bed all day,
But I know I've got to go,
And drag myself to school,
I wait for the bus,
Outside in the cold,
And then the long drive to school,
The school makes me sad,
The school makes me happy,
The school is like a dream,
But I never know if I want to wake up,
I remember in the past,
Some of those days I'll never forget,
And some of those days which go on and on,
When you just want it to stop,
Then the bell you dream of hearing,
The bell that sends you home,
And back into Heaven,
But soon enough it all happens again,
Just like every day,
Just like every normal day.

James Somerville (12)
Collingwood College, Camberley

Something Special

This summer we got a puppy
He means the world to me
We go on lots of long walks
And we named him Tufty

He has a lot of fluffy fur
Especially his head and ears
He runs like a cheetah in the wilderness
It feels as though we've had him years

He plays with me in the garden
And makes me laugh a lot
He leaps on and off the trampoline
And drinks out of the flower pot

When I come in from a day at school
He jumps right up at me
Not being naughty
Just with lots of glee

I wanted to do this rhyme
So I can share my feelings with you
I hope one day you find
Something as special too.

Daniella Hawes (12)
Collingwood College, Camberley

The Streets

Days pass,
Ever so slowly,
Living still always lonely,
Weeks pass and I've lost track,
From when my mother turned her back,
She left so soon and she left so quietly,
Like a mouse creeping in anxiety,
She was scared she was,
Of something out there,
On the streets.

I lay at night,
Watching the door,
Hoping she is scared no more,
To come and hold me and give me comfort.

I heard a footstep,
I freeze in bed,
Beads of sweat dripping down my head,
I was scared I was,
Of something out there,
On the streets.

James Baxter (12)
Collingwood College, Camberley

Chocolate Cake

Friends are like chocolate cake,
you can never have too many.
Chocolate cake
is like Heaven, always amazing you,
each taste, full of feeling.
Chocolate cake
is like life, with so many different pieces.
Chocolate cake
is like happiness,
you can never get enough of it.

Rahul Jassi (13)
Collingwood College, Camberley

Irritating Habits

Most irritating habits?
Keeping clean. All that effort.
Jay would never forget her anti-bacterial sprays.
I wonder if she's ever considered spraying me.

Or if I'd ever find a substitute for the word 'uhm'
Orals? The worst, mainly because of the word.
But it's better in groups
The horrific soundless moments
Are shared between us

Unlike when I'm in the mall, alone, with 'An-Meri'
Whose calling of the nickname 'Nunski'
Is a personal nuisance
And public embarrassment.

Talking too much? Could be.
For what's in my mind, I do speak,
So the traitors I call my sisters
Are probably out to get me
For the snitching I've done is the most irritating.

Ama Uris (16)
Collingwood College, Camberley

Friendship Poem

You're a friend who's always there,
You're the one who always cares,
You're the one who stands by me,
When times get tough,
It makes it easy when life gets rough,
I could never lose you in the end,
I don't know what life would be like,
If I didn't have you as a friend,
So the real truth is, I need you till the end,
You're my very best friend
And you will stick by me until the very end!

Amber Shelby Ellen Angol (13)
Collingwood College, Camberley

Netball

Standing, with your arms outstretched
You see nothing but the ball, everything else is a blur.
You feel like giving up,
Like falling down
But you know that you won't let yourself.

You feel the presence of the ball,
It's in sight,
It's coming towards you.
See yourself catching it,
Be the ball,
Feel it.
This is the only moment that matters.
Everything stops.

You have caught the ball.
Suddenly, you are back in reality.
You hear the roaring crowd, you see the energetic players.
You are back in reality,
And you must succeed.

Zoe Fawcett (12)
Collingwood College, Camberley

Daddy's Girl

It's the time of Snow White and the Seven Dwarfs
I'm playing in my room and then he calls
I run down like a cheetah - really fast
My sister smiles as she walks past
He's back home from work; it's been a hard day
He gives me a hug and a kiss and I go back to play
He gave me his eyes, he made me, me
I'm so happy he's my dad, can't you see

Today is the day of the cross country run
I run past the last corner, having so much fun
Then I hear his voice calling my name
He's always so proud of me, I'm so glad he came
I'm pushing and pushing to make him proud
Still hear him screaming loud, loud, loud
I cross the finish line so tired, feeling dead
He runs up to me, takes me in his arms and kisses my head
His hugs are as cosy as a big fluffy bear
We both treasure our close friendship with lots of care.

Jessica Pass (13)
Collingwood College, Camberley

My Ride

Rolling over the hills
In my custom wheels
Fresh cold air
Flowing through my hair

With no time for wasting
I raced along to Hastings
Rooftop down
Crusin' slowly through town

Feeling mean, riding on 18's
Two-tone paint shines and gleams

Rock to the bass
Smile on my face
Riding with my crew
In my 2+2

This is my weekend
It's what I love to do.

Liam Bone (14)
Collingwood College, Camberley

Family

Family. It's like a puzzle.
When all the pieces are together it looks stunning.
Full of love, and it shines so bright,
But if you lose one of those pieces, the light fades on that corner.

As we stand here today, we remember,
Remember who she was and what she has done.
The joy and laughter will live on in us;
We still have a part to play here.

The path Eileen has now taken is just another part of life
And when you find it, that sunrise and silver clouds, embrace you.
We stand around here and the sun will shine!
The puzzle pieces will be replaced, with joy and happiness.

The light will return.
This is not the end, this is the life of our family,
It will never end.
Strength and honour.

Greg Payne (15)
Collingwood College, Camberley

The Rap About Me

I'm a dark ceaser
With a bad fever
Please follow the leader

Hey now, be fresh
I know it's in my flesh
You don't have to be like that
'Cause you can chat
Unlike a bat

Too much food
Gets me in a mood
'Cause I'm a dark ceaser
With a bad fever.

Shayan Khorsheed (12)
Copland Community College, Wembley

Why Choose Crime?

Every day you hear about another shooting
Boys getting shot for the colour that they're wearing
Girls getting clocked
For the way that they're acting
Chains being snatched
For the hustling that's happening.

But why choose crime?
Got a nice home and a family that love you
Doing bad things, to see your parents cry
I suppose when you're gone, they might as well die
All the things that you do are affecting your family.

Coming home late at night
Nobody knows, 'Where are you?'
But all I have to say
Why choose crime?
Crime's not a good thing
Your life can end
Be put in a jail cell or maybe even dead
Try to take in the poem, that I wrote today
'Cause many youths die from the words that I say!

Rochelle Mcleod (13)
Copland Community College, Wembley

Crime

Gun crime, knife crime everywhere,
Even though you might get scared, be aware,
Of the dangers you may face,
Even if you're just going out with a few mates.

This might not go through your little head but just try to understand
What many others can,
That the streets aren't always safe,
They're even worse when it is black and late.

Yasmin Mohammed
Copland Community College, Wembley

Untitled

The engine of a Lamborghini
The horsepower of a Porsche
Taking in so much speed
That's a lot of force

Being in a supercar as it reaches top speed
0 to 60 under 4 seconds, jeez!
A V12 engine working as hard as it can
So much torque it sounds like a man

A Zonda F has 520 brake horsepower
That's a top speed of 215 miles per hour
The masterpiece of the Audi R8
The intelligence of a Maclaren F1
That's not something you want to drive around town in
To go and pick up your mum.

There is lots of technology being put into cars
They will soon find out how to get them to Mars
Inside a Lamborghini driving down a Swiss mountain
Watching the water rush down like a fountain.

Jerome Lake (13)
Copland Community College, Wembley

The Sparkling Star

T here always
H as to be a star
E very star, any star

S hining beautifully in the sky
P roud
A nd
R olling in every direction trying to
K eep the sky bright at night
L oving each and every one
I n a special kind of way
N ot knowing who to shine on every
G reat day

S parkling into everyone's eyes
T empting to be touched
A lways
R ising by night and hiding by day and
sooner than later, on its way.

Shivani Gohu
Copland Community College, Wembley

Writer's Block

W riter's block,
R eading and writing,
I nformation disappearing,
T imeless thinking gone to waste,
E very second just wondering what to write,
R ewriting every single word,
S till nothing comes to mind.

B rains whirring,
L onging to think of something,
O nly nothing can be written down,
C ompletely unaware of my surroundings,
K nowing now that you've got . . . writer's block!

Alanya-Jessica Johnstone (13)
Copland Community College, Wembley

Winter

Winter is very cold,
It's what I've been told.
How it shimmers to the ground,
It makes such a lovely sound.

Winter is a great season,
I will tell you the reason.
Because of all the snowmen,
I made at least ten.

Father Christmas comes on a winter's day,
Everybody says, 'Hooray!'
In winter, I play out, until late,
With my best friend, Kate.

All I have to say,
Is that winter is the best day.
Winter is phenomenal,
It makes my happiness go eternal.

Sofian Chaibi (12)
Copland Community College, Wembley

Teen Stuff

Teens watch TV,
Especially the BBC,
Girls use the phone,
While their mums and dads moan,
Boys play football,
To them it's really skilful,
Some have their own band,
And some want to have their own land,
The girls spend Dad's money
And the boys try to act funny.

We're teens
What do you expect?

Angel Shannon Brogan
Copland Community College, Wembley

Poor And Rich

All over the globe
There are poor and rich countries
People in poverty
People with much money
If we'd come together
Imagine how we'd be
Africa, Asia, North America
South America, Europe
All over the globe.

People are buying
While there's ones who are dying.

There are people in isolation
While we're going to parties
With invitations.

Abukar Abukar (12)
Copland Community College, Wembley

Ways To Stop Getting Bored

Watch your favourite soaps
Play a prank on a brother or sister
Put Ice cream down their back
Or maybe listen to your favourite track.

Bake something for your mother
A cake, some delicious buns
Just to have a little bit of fun.

Go out with a bunch of friends
Go play hockey or football
Or maybe the mall.

Now you know what to do
Why sit at home like a lonely kangaroo
Just get up and jump!

Madhvi Patel (12)
Copland Community College, Wembley

Brap, Brap

Brap, brap, act cool on the bus,
Brap, brap, you don't know about us,
Brap, brap, walk to school,
Brap, brap, don't act like a fool.

Every time I want to have fun with my mates,
Out the house and through the garden gates,
Hop on my bike or even grab a ball I can peddle,
I can dribble all the way to school.

Brap, brap, act cool on the bus,
Brap, brap, you don't know about us,
Brap, brap, walk to school,
Brap, brap, don't act like a fool.

Brap, brap.

Ralford Thorpe (12)
Copland Community College, Wembley

My Sweet Not Sour Mum

Mum there is nothing sweeter than you,
Not even hot cocoa on a cold day too.
Not even ice cream or all the cakes in the world,
There is nothing better, it's true there is nothing sweeter than you.

Sometimes I think you are sour,
But you get sweeter every hour.
You help me out when I am filled with power,
You say you love me every hour.

You might think I am sour but even if I really am sour,
I will always love you, every hour.
I love you my sweet not sour mum.

Chenai James (12)
Copland Community College, Wembley

Goodbye

She was unwanted as an old doll
As silent as death.
I felt her emotions as Tina, Alice and Joe walked away,
Bullied, tortured, lonely. Goodbye.

Bitten by the poison of the bullies.
Attacked by the cruelness of life.
Her poor heart was breaking slowly.
Shouting, hurting, a black eye. Goodbye.

Rosetta is different, so what?
We still belong together.
God made us different for a reason.
Tears, silence, cries. Goodbye.

Katherine Reynolds (11)
De Stafford School, Caterham

Walking Along Nature's Path

The morning dew may kiss
The emerald grass.
The blooming flowers kiss
The golden sun.

The birds are chirping away,
Awaiting their eggs to hatch
As the fisherman sitting by the lake
Waiting for something to catch.

Dark clouds are rolling in
It is time for a shower.
Boom! The thunder booms
And opens up a path to Heaven.
Crash! The lightning dances
Majestically across the once blue sky.

Drip, drop, drip, drop,
The rain is falling.

Daisy Lawrence (12)
Epsom & Ewell High School, West Ewell

The Dragon

The wind swishes angrily,
The rain patters down.
As from inside a little village,
The chief shivered and frowned.

The villagers looked worried,
As they heard a scream of agony.
Not a deer or a hare,
But human that's not free.

A minute passed . . .
An hour passed . . .
As a metallic stench was found,
The ground starts to sweat.
But not any sweat,
A lukewarm liquid from who was dead.
No other colour than red.

The villagers looked nervously,
As they had sent a scout for food.
They heard a snap of bones,
As their hope diminished from their mood.

I finish this poem with the relief for you,
That the villagers survived the pain.
They hunted the creature,
To find it to be a grand dragon.

Its scales shimmered gold,
Its eyes glowered silver.
I hope to meet this creature,
Once and for all.

Hail Kim (11)
Epsom & Ewell High School, West Ewell

War

It was the final stand,
The bombs fell like lightning,
Date was 1/1/12,
That's when it happened.

Crash! Boom! Bash!

The drop pods fell,
They were here,
'It's them!'
I said.

As fast as I could,
I turned and ran in a flash,
It was too late, slime had me,
Around the throat . . .

I was afraid,
Petrified,
The aliens took me,
Into their ship.

The predator spat at me,
With white spit,
And pushed me in the corner,
The last thing I saw.
My own blood!

It was the end,
Of the world,
Of humanity,
Of me.

David Sims (11)
Epsom & Ewell High School, West Ewell

As Cool As A Cucumber

As cool as a cucumber
As sweet as honey
As blistering as a sunny day
As shiny as money

As cheeky as a monkey
As bubbly as a bath
As fruity as a fruit bowl
As funny as a laugh

As arty as an artist
As loud as a screaming child
As musical as a musician
As fierce as a lion in the wild

As bouncy as a ball
As pointy as a pin
As stupid as a fool
As disgusting as a bin

As hard as a slap
As yellow as mustard
As handy as a map
As runny as custard

As cool as a cucumber
As sweet as honey
As blistering as a sunny day
As shiny as money.

Megan Martin (11)
Epsom & Ewell High School, West Ewell

Reading

I'm sitting at my desk,
I'm still, comfortable

I'm in World War II,
Guns are shooting,
People are shouting,
The fear is growing.

I'm in a magical garden,
The fear drains away,
The beauty is immense,
Butterflies floating by,
I don't want to leave.

Whoosh!
I'm on the back of a luminous dragon,
The prodigious creature's swooping like the wind,
My heart is racing with excitement,
The crowd is cheering me on.

I'm on a ship,
It is large and creaky,
The crew are running,
The fear is back,
The captain shouts . . .

'Dinner's ready!'
I put down my book,
And race downstairs.

Dani-Mai Barton (11)
Epsom & Ewell High School, West Ewell

What He Means To Me

When I saw his gleaming face in the sun,
Looking up at me with his bold smile,
His green shiny shell placed on his back,
That's what made me understand what he means to me.

His bright sparkling eyes looked straight at me,
He was glowing so much it nearly blinded me,
His brilliant shade of green,
That's what made me understand what he means to me.

When he walks through the big grass,
It makes me feel how small he is,
I wonder what made me understand how much he meant to me.

Crunch!
That is the sound of him eating his lettuce,
Splash!
That is the sound of him diving into his shallow pool of water,
That's what made me understand how much he meant to me.

I wonder what it's like to be him,
Walking over his rocks and logs,
Being admired by the world,
I wonder, I wonder, I wonder.

He may not mean anything to you,
But in my heart he means the entire world to me,
That's why he's my little tortoise.

Emma Cronk (11)
Epsom & Ewell High School, West Ewell

Decision Time

The noises of plates and cutlery,
That drives us insane,
The discussion of ideas and plans,
Places to visit are hard to name,
A large plate arrives and we dig in,
Memories of the past come up a lot,
Some people never change,
Dessert is offered but we say bill,
The last clash of glasses and we are off.
Arriving at the car bravely they say . . .
Back to mine or another day,
Yeah alright,
In the car we're all excited,
Not too much I guess but we're still delighted,
At their house, cake and wine is offered to the primes
Which means we're still having Coke,
The younger kids get fidgety and start to poke,
My parents interfere with the conclusion made at the table
And they baffle their way to a happier tale!
The evening was long and we're heading home,
We get back and we're drained to the bone,
Bed seems a dream and we are all tired but sleeping is hard . . .
Knowing we are going to California next week.

Louisa Mills (12)
Epsom & Ewell High School, West Ewell

Cheetah

Its elegance and grace as it races after its prey
Then it stops to camouflage in the long thick grass
It pounces on to the prey and rips its flesh from bone
Like chainsaws shredding through velvet
It summons its cubs
And they masticate on the ruins of the dead creature.

Ben Burlinson (11)
Epsom & Ewell High School, West Ewell

Anyone Can Be A Superhero

Anyone can be a superhero
Everyone thinks that superheroes are men dressed in tights
With super powers and always save the day.
Anyone can be a superhero
Even you!

To be a superhero all it takes is a little faith and courage
To succeed in life and to be loved and cherished by everyone.
If you're a hero people look up to you
And when they grow up they want to be just like you
To be a hero you need to put effort into everything you ever do or say.
Every step you take you are confident and proud
You are independent but also like the company
A real hero makes the right decisions and think things through
They know how to solve problems
They love what they are
And everyone else
They care about other people

There are people walking down the street that are heroes
Some people don't realise it yet
Are you a hero?
Anyone can be a superhero!

Hollie Desave (11)
Epsom & Ewell High School, West Ewell

My Girlies!

I have many friends,
But these are the best.
They always keep my secrets,
They're better than the rest!

Jess is a superstar,
Abbie loves her wine.
Holly is a great laugh,
Can you believe they're mine?

Louisa is beautiful,
And really, really smart.
Radha is polite,
And has a big heart!

Kirsty is a stunner,
And hyper all the time.
Whereas Lauren likes to be quiet,
And makes herself shine!

Well I hope you like my friends,
I know that I do!
If you don't have friends like mine,
Then I feel sorry for you!

Emma Seldon (12)
Epsom & Ewell High School, West Ewell

My Dad

Sit back and reminisce just for a minute
And ask yourself, can you really feel it
Taken from the mind of a blessed and loved one
When he woke from his sleep I was no longer his son
He took his time to try and remember me
And the rest of his heartbroken family
Déjà vu was all he could remember
Tears of frustration filled his face
Turns out he didn't win the race

When I was young they used to be happy
My mum, my dad and the rest of my family
But then he left and made terrible decisions
And my mum gave me weird messed-up visions
At the age of ten, I began to see him again
Eight years of progress, he finally saw me
Took him long enough, I thought he'd ignore me

So that's the story of me and my dad
For a lot of my life he made me go mad
But then he made an effort and slipped me a smile
I hope he stays with me for more than a while.

Frankie Nicholson (11)
Epsom & Ewell High School, West Ewell

Snow

She is soft as a bunny
And as quiet as the sea,
When you look out of your window
She isn't hard to see.

She lies in your garden
Like a white soft blanket for all to see.
But sometimes she is cruel
And as nasty as a storm,
But when she goes, she's gone.

Chloe Harrington (11)
Epsom & Ewell High School, West Ewell

Bright And Sunny

A bright summer's day,
The water falls,
From the river,
Flowing beautifully and elegantly,
Through the forest.

The sunlight shining through,
The rustling green leaves of the trees,
Looks like an angel coming down from Heaven,
As beautiful as can be.

Walking through the forest,
With my mum and dad,
The fabulous pitter-patter,
From the water,
Repeating again and again.

The place I went,
Was the best place ever,
I wish I could go there,
For ever and ever.

Abbie McMaster (11)
Epsom & Ewell High School, West Ewell

The Desert

It's so hot.
The sweat goes down on my face
Like rain goes down on the window.
I can hear the birds sing a lovely song.
I go on the shady trees for some fresh air.
There isn't any noise,
So I can close my eyes and relax.
This place is so quiet!
The sea is calm and small waves
Make a lovely sound.

I hope that this place will never fade.

Natasha Anjoree (11)
Epsom & Ewell High School, West Ewell

Peacock

It's beautiful,
Standing there.
Multicoloured hair,
Eyeing me,
But silently
Standing.

Tanned brown, blue, green,
Always keeps itself clean.
Turquoise, golden yellow
Always mellow.

But still beautiful,
And standing there.
Little eyes,
But long hair.

Bye-bye,
See you again.
Hope I'll see my multi-coloured friend,
Again.

Lauren Evans (12)
Epsom & Ewell High School, West Ewell

War

Captured!
I have been captured by Hitler and his men.
Hitler told me something in German.
Ich werde dich töten und nicht, something horrible.
I couldn't speak German so I didn't know what he said.
I tried to get away, all of a sudden, *bang!*
All I felt was a liquid dripping down my leg,
Drip, drip, drip!
It was the sound of dripping blood,
My blood!
I screamed for my life . . .

Cian Melia (11)
Epsom & Ewell High School, West Ewell

A Day At School

In the playground the children are having fun,
The bell goes and they all start to run,
As the lesson starts to begin,
The children pile in.

The lesson begins to end,
The teachers start to send,
The children out to play,
Because it's a lovely day.

As the children wait out of PE,
Everyone apart from me,
As I am not feeling very well,
After PE all the boys smell.

As the school day begins to end,
I rush to the post box with a letter to send,
As I push my key through the door,
There is a letter on the floor.

Holly Banks (12)
Epsom & Ewell High School, West Ewell

Snow

Groan, Wednesday morning, school again,
I get up, get dressed,
Wake my family up
And go and open the curtains;
I notice something white and fluffy in the corner of my eye,
I look back out of the window;
And shout from the top of my voice,
'Snow! No school!'
Immediately my sister gets dressed,
She runs straight up to my mum and dad and begs,
'Can we make a snowman?'
My mum and dad look at each other and grin,
My sister rushes to get her gloves and scarf on and runs outside,
Falling face first in the snow.
She calls my name and asks me to get a carrot and some chocolate.
The snowman is complete.
Winter fun until the summer comes along.

Sophie Bassett (12)
Epsom & Ewell High School, West Ewell

The School Poem

Children chatting while running to lessons
As the loud school bell rings
The children eventually get to their lesson
As you hear pencils and pens scratch on the books and paper.
At break time the fresh air rings around the school
As if it was a doorbell.
The playground and field full of teachers
Telling playful kids to behave when lining up for the next lesson.
The smells of freshly baked muffins ring around the canteen
After the muffins have gone.
Teachers eager to get the remaining muffins.
Children gossiping while walking out of the school gates
After a long busy day at Epsom and Ewell High School
With the children's heads up high,
Happy with the big orange super slip in their pockets.

Jack Stringer (12)
Epsom & Ewell High School, West Ewell

Winter

Two minutes before home time,
I have been watching the clock tick and tock
For at least half an hour now,
All I want to do is get out and see the pale snow
Gradually make its way to the ground,
The teacher sets the homework.
I put my head upon the desk,
Tired of listening so we all have a rest,
The teacher is done so we head for the door,
She tells us to wait but we can't take anymore.

We're finally outside and everyone else is too,
People ducking from snowballs and hiding from the cold,
The day is over so we all head home,
This has been a laugh, it will never get old.

Sasha-Jade Martin (12)
Epsom & Ewell High School, West Ewell

Battle Of The Somme

The day was dim, the moon had risen,
It was time of rest,
The father lazing on some hay,
Listened to his son's request.

'Why, oh why,' the son did ask
'Are the fields so dark
And their grass so tattered?'
Said the father to the son,
''Tis the bones of the Brits that here lie scattered.'

''Twas once a battle of great debacle,
In which young men were led to fight,
Against evil and vile and all things hostile,
Young men were led to fight.'

The son looked up, and waited,
But when no reply had come,
The son did ask, 'Tell me about this fight,
And why it left such a hurtful blight.'

''Twas General Haig that said,
'Fear not young men, for what I have to say,
Is that you stroll across this no-man's-land;
On this sunny day'

And though the Brits parade towards,
The manned machines of Hell,
They sing their final chords as they
Begin to shout and yell.

If you would ask the whereabouts of General Haig,
You'd find him behind the old trench wall,
Hiding from the plague.
But if all that you seek is the private from the Shire,
Then look no further, he's there on the old barbed wire.'

As the father concluded,
He looked down at his son,
The son looked up,
With hungry eyes,
'You told me about this human treason

But now I ask you, what was the reason?

Said the father to the son:
'For that I cannot say, my dear,
But what I can recite,
Is that on that sunny summer's day,
Young men were led to fight.'

John Russell (16)
Farnham Heath End School, Farnham

Home

Night never comes in this jungle of ours,
The neon doesn't burn out,
But the stars have,

We can't be equal,
You're all too prejudice,
The windows get too high,
So do your egos,

With ghosts who stumble,
But never slumber,
Forever entwined with the traffic's endless flow,

Your paranoia and knives,
Insanity thrives,
The curtains remain open,
This show's never over,

Nobody is able to take their time,
Looking for places to seek cheap thrills and fun,
This world of madness is set forever,
Unbroken by the sun,

Take a step back,
See the world through a child's eyes,
Screams come in through the window,
He pulls up the sheets,
It seems human rights don't live on these streets.

James Anthony Traylen (14)
Farnham Heath End School, Farnham

My Story

Look at them over there
So vibrant, so cool
Those red curtains
Make my bed sheets look a fool

Then we move onto the window
So square, so transparent
Out of the window
The world is apparent

I see the rich boy
James is his name
PS3 for Christmas
The Game Boy I got was lame

The parting of his hair
Might as well be ginger
Loser, weird, fool, rich
Definitely not a ninja

It then dawns on me
Everyone bullying him
So I tried to stop
Now I bully Tim.

Then Tim beats me up
Punches me in the mouth
I then say to his girlfriend
Don't worry, I'm not going south

I found a miniature schnauzer
Bingo was his name
A stupid, silly poem
Somehow gets him fame

It's the end of my story
Hey I'm a poet and I didn't know it.

Russell Golding (14)
Farnham Heath End School, Farnham

What It's Really Like

The sound of guns
Explosion of grenades
As the infantry runs
Osama Bin Laden, renegades
Broken walls
Craters in the field
The general calls
Their guns they yield

Pull the pin
Pull the trigger
It's not a sin
If you shoot that figure
Paint on your face
Boots on your feet
Waiting at the base
Armed and dangerous and won't accept defeat

In the air
On the ground
War isn't fair
Be careful, don't make a sound
When it is done
And all is dead
War isn't fun
It's miserable instead.

Ryan Larby (13)
Farnham Heath End School, Farnham

Remembered With Honour

Do not leave, my dear, I beg of you,
Stay with me just one more night.
I need you more than they, my love,
I could not live if you were to die.

I must go, my love, to fight for my country,
Though I shall miss you more than life itself,
But on the day that I return,
How much sweeter your kiss shall taste,
How more valuable your touch,
So sweet and gentle.

But what am I to do,
While you are out fighting for our world?
Am I to just sit and wait for your return,
To idle away my time, when you may not come back at all?

My dear, rest your frantic nerves.
Remember, I fight not for my world,
I fight for you, and all I love.
And remember, my sweet, if my body is to waste away,
I have died defending what is right,
And I shall know as I lie in the mud,
I shall be remembered with honour,
And spoken of with pride.

Annie Farthing (13)
Farnham Heath End School, Farnham

Paper Of Tales

The paper of tales were not cold and crumpled
but new, like a freshly pressed shirt.

The pages smelt and felt familiar,
not musty and rough, but sweet and soft.

The tales were expressed with feelings of happiness,
smiles and laughter
until . . .

A gust of wind lifted the paper of tales from the table top,
twisting and turning, dancing and swaying,
down . . .
down . . .
down . . .
floating to the ground.

Rustled by the breeze but settled in the trees,
the birds ripped to shreds the happy tales.

Singing them to their young in the depth of the forest,
the paper of tales are now gone.

Alma Sargeant (12)
Farnham Heath End School, Farnham

Fields Of Death

Trudging through fields of death,
as I try to hold in my suffering breath.

Walking in my rotten boots,
through broken fences and tree trunk roots.

Wounded soldiers with missing limbs,
smell like trash cans and plastic bins.

Cuts, grazes and many, many scars,
lay beneath the shattered stars.

I hate the world, the shameful violence,
a gunshot hits me, I fall with silence.

Caitlin Forbes (13)
Farnham Heath End School, Farnham

Victims

Every day, every night,
All I get is nasty spite,
Thoughts go through my head,
Even when I go to bed.

When I get to school,
All they do is follow me to the hall,
I walk, I run,
And they threaten me with a gun.

I scream, I yell,
And there goes the fire bell,
I hate you so,
Because you smell of BO.

I tell my dad, I tell my mum,
They just sigh and call them scum,
I start to cry and say goodbye,
I can't bear
But I thought they were there.

Eden Canarn (14)
Farnham Heath End School, Farnham

Love

Love, like a never-ending waterfall
Love, a new beginning for someone special
Love, a commitment to one another
Love, like watching two swans making a heart shape
Love, the warm feeling on Valentine's Day
Love, the endless feeling of happiness
Love, the feeling that you shall never part
Love, the passion that binds two people together
Love, like you are a princess at a ball
Love, the little piece of hope that stays with you every day
Love life as you shall love one another.

Michelle Westbrook (13)
Farnham Heath End School, Farnham

Finding A Heart Of Gold

Stranded. Lonely. No more fish in the sea,
Blinded. Sorrow. What was wrong with me?
Track marks. Crying. Take back what I said,
Broken-hearted. Part of me's dead.

I found you. You lost me. How'd you think I feel?
Deserted. Painful. And I thought it was real.
Wasted. Mourning. All love's gone cold.
Happy ending. Not what they told.

I love you. Ignore me. Make me feel like this,
Promise. Broken. No time to think.
Fight it. Lose it. Love's gone with the wind,
Forever. Begging. To me you sinned.

Over. Darkness. You're more than upset.
Would it? Could it? Turn to a regret?
Help me. Help you. Be the one to hold;
Take me. Keep me. Find your heart of gold.

Oliver Wearing (13)
Farnham Heath End School, Farnham

Summer Evening

A great dark bird silhouetted against the dim light of the evening sky,
A lonely mouse scuttles cautiously across a dull grey path,
A sly mother fox sneaks reluctantly from her den of young,
A soft musky rabbit makes a faint shadow on the crest of a grassy hill,
A painted moth delicately flaps his wings
As he floats past a waving beech bough,
It softly gets darker as the evening merges to night
And the stars peek out,
And I stare longingly through the misty window,
Watching everything from my room.

Lizzy Tatarek (11)
Farnham Heath End School, Farnham

War Poem

The clap of guns,
The smell of fear,
The fallen soldiers lying near
The dirt, the grime, the rats and rubbish.
The sights and sounds too real to publish,
Cos never could a written word describe a horror this absurd.
The blood and tears, am I in Hell?
I guess I'm not but might as well.
What I would give to not have seen,
This world of pain, and heard the screams.
And look into your brothers' eyes,
As cold and terrified as they die.
The hope for peace is more a dream,
A distant one, at that it seems.
The enemies are people too,
But you kill them and they kill you.

Beth Dyson (13)
Farnham Heath End School, Farnham

Mother Nature's Massacre

In the blazing heat of a quiet day,
The ground beneath the town begins to shake,
Civilisation refuses to stay.
Houses sink as lives shatter in the quake.
Piercing screams of the young, the old, the ill,
A cloud of dust rises over the town.
Nations watch with baited breath and no will,
Hopes, dreams and Haiti come crashing down.
Aid is slow to reach this God forsaken place.
Lives are torn by the sharp, jagged rubble.
People wander with many a haunted face.
The desperate drifting, causing trouble.
The graves of the dead line the lonely road.
The strength of nature, we have been shown.

Laura Palmer (14)
Farnham Heath End School, Farnham

The Day She Never Left

Her eyes are looking into my soul
When she moves to me my heart skips a beat
She leaves . . . my heart will fall into a hole
When she walks she glows like the burning sun
Tears run down my face, time to say goodbye
My life is broken into tiny pieces
As she leaves the glowing begins to shy
Crying, her heart broken in two
My hand stretches out to touch that of hers
She turns, eyes welled up, I pull her closer
I can feel her heart beating . . . calm my nerves
She turns her head, our lips lovingly touch
I close my eyes, my heart beating faster
We look at each other, burst into laughter.

Mason King (14)
Farnham Heath End School, Farnham

I Love Food

It is wonderful when I grate my cheese.
When I spread my butter on my wholemeal!
It makes me really happy, and I freeze.
Gravy and chips, makes a tasty, nice meal.
Why do Monster Munch crisps, make my breath smell?
Why is Marks & Spencers' food so special?
My Babybel cheese, is like a big shell.
I wipe my food surface with my Dettol.
Doritos are so orange and cheesy.
My smooth Galaxy bars make me chill out.
If I eat too much it makes me queasy.
If someone takes the last Freddo I will shout.
I love food.
It is good.

Cody Moir (13)
Farnham Heath End School, Farnham

War Poem

I'm on the ground, just lying down
The gas is causing me to drown.
I cannot see through the smoke
And now I start to choke and choke.
I cannot stop, I cannot start
Blood is going from my heart
Although I know I have to stay
There is no more I can say
I close my eyes and start to shudder
I just hope this happens to no other.

Laura Greenhill (14)
Farnham Heath End School, Farnham

Broken Hearts

Broken,
A million little pieces,
Just like that

Smashed,
Confidence no longer lingers,
I'm afraid

Love,
One word, so many meanings,
Blissfully happy

Forever,
We were supposed to be together,
Together forever

Heartbroken
Not the first time,
Definitely not the last.

Lily Pettett (14)
Fullbrook School, Addlestone

Spring

Spring blossoming through the winter,
while the excitement of Christmas, New Year and snowy days melt away.
Back to school. Back to reality.

When I think of spring, it reminds me of the Easter holiday.
A little girl waking up on Easter Sunday.
Running downstairs, with my brother at my side,
scanning the house for what I could find.
Chocolate eggs left just for me,
from the wonderfully magic Easter Bunny.
Back then I was so wide-eyed,
believing anything I'd hear.
Now I am knowing and the magic is not there.

When I think of spring, it reminds me of my family.
My mum's birthday and my parents' anniversary.
Of all the great memories, here and there,
going out for dinner, finding something to wear.
Making breakfast in bed and it all going wrong,
'It's the thought that counts,' my mum said all along.
Home-made cards that glitter everywhere,
A home-made cake that just cannot compare!

Not all my memories are so happy,
Easter Monday '06, the sad news had struck me,
my grandad had passed away in the night,
he was kind and caring and ever so bright.
But after all of the sadness, sorrow and tears,
we remembered the good times that we had all shared
in the light summer breeze and the freshened spring air.
Those days he would sit out on his plastic deckchair,
we'd all sit around, my family and me.
And those are some of my most cherished memories.

Everyone says spring is a fresh start,
a season filled with hope, prospect, ambition,
but for me, spring is remembering.
Remembering a time where anything is possible;
remembering wonderful family moments;
remembering someone really special to me.

Emma Carr (13)
Fullbrook School, Addlestone

The Last Of Its Kind

1,000 years ago and a day,
a wizard cast a spell,
upon a baby dragon who,
had drunk from out his well.

The spell he put upon the beast,
was the worst that he could find,
to sleep throughout a thousand years,
and then to wake up kind.

The beast when he awoke,
had slept for many years,
he found he was the last,
and burst into tears.

Just then a fearless knight rode past,
and heard the dragon's roar,
he was fairly shaken,
and dismayed by what he saw.

The knight went to the king,
and he was very upset,
'Good king,' the knight cried,
'there's hope for us yet.'

The knight was quaking in his boots,
as he crouched low in the grass,
tense with expectation,
waiting for the dragon to pass.

The dragon was sitting in the grass,
tears of sadness creeping down his snout,
as he watched the river ripple and wave,
and the mackerel, salmon and trout.

The dragon flew aimlessly,
getting closer to the knight,
not watching the ground,
a miraculous sight!

The knight was still as a mouse,
one false move and he was dead,
down would come the dragon,

and off with his head.

His spear left his hand,
it pierced the dragon's heart,
he fell straight as an arrow
and quick as a dart.

The dragon was dead,
the knight had triumphed,
but the spirit lives on,
of the last of its kind.

Dragons aren't cruel, just defensive,
this shows how cruel humans really are.

Judith Wood (11)
Fullbrook School, Addlestone

Weekends

Weekends are really cool
Staying up late, better than ten to eight

In the morning I stay in bed
I don't have to worry about my bed head

Morning TV, that's something for me
That really makes me happy

I like to play on my PlayStation
After my eggs and bacon

I enjoy my time with my family
Especially watching something on the telly

Here is my favourite time of the day
Not time to play but dinner on my plate.

Sam Wells (11)
Fullbrook School, Addlestone

My Pet Cat

I have a pet cat
She is called Lulu
She is very scared of bats
And loves to wear hats.

I have a pet cat
She is called Lulu
She cleans the mat
And likes to play bat.

I have a pet cat
She is called Lulu
Always fat
And always sleeps on the mat.

I have a pet cat
She is called Lulu
Loves to brush her teeth
But never neat.

I have a pet cat
She is called Lulu
Loves to play with Paul
But always drools.

I have a pet cat
She is called Lulu
She always has muddy paws
Never tidies up her drawers.

Tilly Roberts (11)
Fullbrook School, Addlestone

Summer

I love the days of summer,
The bright hot air,
Driving past without a care,
Making us sweat in our game,
Without a doubt that we're lame,
Because,
It's summer!

I love the nights of summer,
The cool, hot summer breeze,
Passing on that smell of cheese,
Catching us all in a doze,
And after all, I suppose,
It's summer!

I love the rest of summer,
Where it is very peaceful,
Because sleeping is the bull,
But the cool, hot summer breeze doesn't rest,
Because it's at its very best,
Because,
It's summer!

I love summer,
You can relax in the cool, hot summer breeze,
After all,
It's summer!

Connor Williams (11)
Fullbrook School, Addlestone

My Limerick

I know this little old lady,
She's deaf and going crazy,
She sits in her home,
Giving sweets to the gnome,
Thinking it's her granddaughter, Amy.

Amy Salt (11)
Fullbrook School, Addlestone

When Frankenstein Was Just A Kid

When Frankenstein was just a kid,
he ate his greens. It's true. He did!
He ate his spinach, salads, peas,
asparagus and foods like these,
and with each leaf and bean
his skin became a bit more green.

On chives and chard he loved to chew,
and Brussels sprouts and peppers too,
until he ate that fateful bean
that turned his skin completely green.
He turned all green, and stayed that way,
and now he frightens folks away.

Poor Frankenstein, his tale is sad,
but things need not have been so bad.
It's fair to say, if only he
had eaten much less celery,
avoided cabbage, ate no kale,
why, then, we'd have a different tale.

So, Mum and Dad, I'm here to say
please take these vegetables away
or my fate could be just as grim.
Yes, I could end up green like him.
So, Mum and Dad, before we dine,
please give a thought to Frankenstein.

Rory Maguire (11)
Fullbrook School, Addlestone

Rabbit

Growing fluffy brown coats to keep warm in the winter,
Chasing the flies and moths, eating dandelions in the spring,
Hopping through the lush green grass in the summer
But in the autumn I gather up food
To get fat and warm for the winter again.

Lauren Miller (12)
Fullbrook School, Addlestone

The Sea

She shouted at the rocks that stood in her way,
She roared with rage as she swept along,
She sent out an icy stare to the bay,
And she would laugh at anyone who wasn't big and strong.

She runs at the sailors that dare to go near,
She sends the ships down to their doom,
She would sit waiting, then strike fishermen with fear,
And she would bellow out through the gloom.

She would lunge forward in a crashing rage,
And then barge onto the cold and rocky land,
She could enter into abandoned caves,
Never saying 'excuse me' to the sand.

She yelled at possibly everyone,
She spat at the coral that challenged her,
She said the pain had only just begun,
And entangled the seaweed into her lure.

Then strangely she would just lie still off the lands,
And whisper to the fish funny thoughts,
She would say 'sorry' to the sands,
She would say, 'A lesson I have been taught'.

Sarah Austwick (12)
Fullbrook School, Addlestone

Football

There is nothing quite like football,
It is the best thing ever made,
It doesn't matter if you're short or tall,
You get very highly paid.
The aim of the game is to score a goal,
That is made out of a few poles,
There are lots of teams including Liverpool,
And I think they rule,
Unlike Arsenal!

Daniel Littler (11)
Fullbrook School, Addlestone

The Meaning Of Life

Life is like a garden,
A garden full of snow,
Be careful where you tread in it though,
All the snow will go.

The good and the bad snow,
The right and the wrong,
People will never forget it,
Even when it's gone.

You never have time to do things,
Before the snow melts,
But it's important to do it,
Before the rain pelts.

This poem means life is not full of time,
Though sometimes unfair,
Try to cope with it,
Even when it's hard to bear.

Peace and justice,
Love and care,
Time and patience,
All you need is there.

Rebecca Ingram (11)
Fullbrook School, Addlestone

Cheese!

Haloumi, Babybel and Dairylea,
Will make me as happy as can be,
Roquefort, Cheestrings,
These are very lovely things,
Roulé and Brie,
Delicious cheese for me,
Cheddar and Wensleydale,
Will never ever fail!

Georgia Howitt (12)
Fullbrook School, Addlestone

Horses

Banging on the door,
My teeth barging out of place
As I shout for help to the neighbour next door.
My hooves raging for the wild plains.
My legs will never gain
Give up like a machine,
Never-ending in its systems,
I hear the ear pounding shouts for calmness in front of me.
Now I've got angry,
I rear up and catch my breath for the run,
I barge out, knocking the human into the wall
The other side of the block.
I charge for the exit and jump out into the open plains,
Ha, that will show them.

Emilie Swann (11)
Fullbrook School, Addlestone

My Two Fish

I have two fish called Bubbles and Speedy,
Bubbles is golden like the sun,
Speedy is as fast as a greyhound,
They both look at me.

I have two fish called Bubbles and Speedy,
Bubbles glides to the top of the tank,
Speedy relaxes at the bottom of it,
They both collect food with their little mouths.

I have two fish called Bubbles and Speedy,
They are both very lively,
They are fun to look at too,
Their golden colours glow at me!

Emily Kedzie (12)
Fullbrook School, Addlestone

Snowy Days

Pouring out of the grey sky,
Like a silent whisper.
A white sheet drifting by,
A teardrop in my eye.

Coldness lurking in the air,
This rare event I share.
The trees glisten with flecks of white,
Oh what a beautiful sight.

As the snow stops falling,
And the birds start calling.
The snow melts away,
Waiting expectantly to reappear another day.

Katie Thomas (12)
Fullbrook School, Addlestone

The Clouds' Song

I look at the clouds in the sky,
And gaze upon them as they drift on by,
An inspiring piece of natural art,
Each wispy cloud, drifting apart
Like the clouds, my thoughts also drift away
And leaves me dreaming, with nothing to say.
My thoughts take me to a new place,
Away from the horrible realities we have to face,
A painting, is what these clouds are,
They are always not too far,
A quiet beauty in our sky,
The eighth wonder of the world in my eye.

Zaib Nasir (14)
Fullbrook School, Addlestone

The Strange Cat

Not so long ago I saw a strange cat
He wasn't so weird, he had no hat
But when he came over, I gave him a pat
He looked so relaxed . . . but I had to go
I went home but he stayed low
But he still followed me home
Simply because he didn't wanna be alone
I accepted him into my household
As he became more at home
And now he lives with me forever
Oh how he was so clever!

Callum Balharrie (11)
Fullbrook School, Addlestone

Forest

I'm running through the forest,
With my dog, Norris.
I can hear the rustling of the leaves,
Until I trip over on my knees.
I look in front of me,
No one to be seen,
I'm scared, frightened,
I'm nowhere to be seen.

Jennifer Gilbert (12)
Fullbrook School, Addlestone

Guinea Pigs

Guinea pigs are the best,
Although they never seem to need a rest,
They run, run, run and squeak, squeak, squeak,
Until you give them grass - their favourite treat.
They always seem to eat,
But they're vegetarian, so they don't eat meat.
So now you know they're so cool,
You're sure to agree, guinea pigs rule!

Ella Bass (12)
Fullbrook School, Addlestone

Lego

Red, green, yellow, blue.
I've made my favourite Lego crew.

First space police,
Atlantis and Indiana Jones No 1.

I love my Lego,
Lego, Lego, Lego and Lego
Is what I do.

Laurence Morgan (11)
Fullbrook School, Addlestone

Untitled

Sadness is when your smile is turned upside down,
Happiness is when your dreams come true,
Disappointment is when you find out the tooth fairy is not real,
Shock is when the people you love are dishonest to you,
Scared is when you think the nasty side of yourself is going to be unleashed,
Guilt is when you let down your best friend and don't say sorry.

Rebecca Turner (12)
Fullbrook School, Addlestone

Autumn Leaves

The leaves are falling off the trees
All different colours and sizes
All the leaves are on the ground
Rustling because they are excited
Many different leaves coming from the sky
As all the leaves say bye-bye
I go away, sit down and cry.

Natalie Cooper (12)
Fullbrook School, Addlestone

Young And Naive? I Know

Young and naive? I know
But that doesn't make me stupid
I am not oblivious
I am aware and more alert than ever
I am no fool; so don't treat me like one

Young and naive? I know
But that doesn't make me stupid

The rape - you steal what's not yours
The hurt - you abuse with so much joy
The lies - you kill so slowly it's excruciating

I am not oblivious
I see the cry of war
I taste the death of children
I hear the pain of women

I am aware and more alert than ever
Because I'm frightened and scared
But it doesn't make me weak
Only stronger

I am no fool; do not treat me like one
Because I understand

You see, I may be young and naive but *I know*.

Juliet Aminat Hassan-Oladele (15)
Kingsmead School, Enfield

A Day Within A Day

They say it takes a minute to find someone special
An hour to appreciate them
A day to love them
But then an entire lifetime to forget them.

How many times do I need to say it . . . ?
You're my pathway to the light
Always have been, always will be.

You've been right here for me
How I wish you could see
That it's been four years since I met you and
It's been a day since I missed you.

I can't see the sun
I can't see the moon
I'm just lost with an empty world in front of me,
I just wish there was some way to get my personality back.

I'm not me, I'm not the real me
Until two people come back into my life
Two very special people
Animals are free
So why can't I be?

I'm lost with an empty world
In front of me!

Susan Wagstaffe (15)
Kingsmead School, Enfield

My Words

My words are a message to the mind
They're the key to a heart
And the clue in the crime
They're the DNA of life
My words are feelings
Twisted into a puzzle
They're the blood of death
The sign of love
The start of hate
The reason for pain
And the darkness which leads to light
My words are there
In my eyes, my hands, my head
Everywhere, but you can't see it
My words are simple
But so complicated
My words are mine
And only I can treasure it
But my words are readable
And my words are a lesson
My words are here
If you want to listen
My words are powerful
My words are the break to a fall.

Eldem Sakir (15)
Kingsmead School, Enfield

Deeper

I take a breath.
The bubbles rise to the surface.
We go deeper.
Further down I see beautiful fish.

I dive a little more each time.
Bubble, bubble.
I see fish with gleaming scales
Swim past me.

I am feeling the pressure
But it is exciting.
The colourful reef is so near.

I dive a little more each time.
Bubble, bubble.
I see fish with gleaming scales
Swim past me.

I feel like a huge hermit crab.
Everything is so peaceful.
My air is running out.
The pressure is so strong now
So I must return to where I belong.
This is why it is so special.

Nicole O'Dell (13)
Lodge School, Purley

Dear Mr Eagle

Dear Mr Eagle,
Why are you so proud?
If I was you, I would be ashamed
When you look down at me with your head in the clouds.
Can you remember ever letting your dinner go?
Or have you never been nice to someone
Just because you're bigger?
I wonder what you think after you finish your dinner?
Do you ever think how much it hurts?
Miss Bunny.

Dear Miss Bunny,
It's really hard to say,
(But you're just dinner anyway).
To some I am enormous,
And I am the king of the clouds
So who cares what you say?
And no I haven't let my dinner go,
It's not just you I eat,
I eat rats, moles, sometimes crows.
But tell me what it's like,
Looking pathetic down there all alone?
Mr Eagle.

Lily Head (13)
Lodge School, Purley

William

A knock on our door
I go to the door and slowly open it
It is the postman with your letter,
Obviously addressed to you
I sit back down at the old oak table
My gorgeous golden locks bouncing
I glanced at your letter, and surprisingly,
It was addressed to me
How peculiar!
I carefully open your signet ring sealed letter,
And slowly take it out
To my darling Alice,
I do miss you
And I am sure that you feel the same
But I will never see you again . . .
Salty tasting water floods down my rosy cheeks like a waterfall,
In the envelope is a golden heart-shaped locket
Engraved on the front, your name, William,
Inside a note reading:
I love you . . .

Nicole Tatur (13)
Lodge School, Purley

Me And My Brother

Me and my brother like to play
But he likes to play once a day.
Me and my brother work really hard
So my mum and dad can say, 'Shock! Horror!'
Me and my brother love each other
And I will love him for ever and ever.
I will never let him go until he has to go.
Me and him are like best friends,
It will be like that until the very end.

Me and my brother tell jokes together
So that we will laugh forever.
Mum and Dad just smile and watch
And hope the clocks will never stop.
He is a role model for all to see
Especially just for me.
He feels my pain when I am sad
And gives me a hug can't you see.

I love him so much and will keep him in my heart
But I will miss him when he is gone again!

Imani Spooner (13)
Lodge School, Purley

Who Did It?

The man standing watching them
Standing there looking at her brother.
Him and his friend playing on the swings
'Wait, we're going over here.'

'No, no, no!' was her silent scream.

Stay here with me!
The mum called her kids in to dinner
Who turned up?
Only him . . .

'No, no, no!'

'Where is she now?'
'Over on the swings.'
Mum ran over to the window
The swing was going back and forth - empty.
The man did it.

'No, no, no . . . !'

Hollie Streeton (13)
Lodge School, Purley

Mind The Gap!

That's all I ever hear,
When I catch the train to school.
Even when I catch it back.
'Mind the gap!' they say again.
'Mind the gap! Mind the gap!'
I heard it the first time.
'Mind the gap!' they said it again.
As I walked home from school.
'Mind the gap!'
But this time I didn't 'mind the gap'!
Splat went 'mind the gap'!
I would never 'mind the gap' again!

Peta-Ann Kelly (13)
Lodge School, Purley

A Lady Reading A Letter

I was reading a letter,
Hoping he was getting better,
He had been gone so long,
It seems like forever,
I just wanted us to be together.

Sitting here all alone
Without you, in this big house,
My only companion is the silly mouse,
Nibbling at my table cloth.

As I get to the end of the letter
It doesn't seem to be getting better

I wept
And wept
I had a secret
That had to be kept . . .

Or should it be kept . . .

Lily Manning (13)
Lodge School, Purley

Alone

(Inspired by the painting 'Weeping Woman' by Pablo Picasso)

I see you every day as I stroll past
I see your eyes all red and sore
As you cry at the door
I wonder why you are like you are
Once a happy cheerful soul
But now you're broken on the floor
People just look and stare
Where is the woman that was always laughing?
Now all you do is sit and worry
How could you live alone in that big house?
You hair is lank
Your face shattered and cracked!

Emily Broyd (13)
Lodge School, Purley

Poppy The Labradoodle

Poppy is my puppy and I love her very much
She is a very soppy doggy
She also likes to copy

She cries a lot when we leave her
We are worried she might get a fever

She can sometimes be very silly
And also a very smelly puppy

She loves to play, bite and fight
She barks all night

She loves meeting everybody
She also loves eating

Her favourite toy is a pink dog

Really there isn't anything else to say
But Poppy is my puppy
And I love her very much.

Georgia Norman (13)
Lodge School, Purley

Mr Robin Redbreast

Mr Robin Redbreast.
So small and weak.
Bottom of the food chain
But there's one thing about Mr Robin Redbreast
He's a very good dancer.
He can do tango, waltz, flamingo and ballet.
I see him on the bird feeder in a little sequinned jacket.
He dances the waltz on Monday, the tango on Tuesday.
The flamingo on Wednesday and ballet on Thursday.
He dances so elegantly like a swan.
But when he's doing the flamingo he's on fire.
I tried to enter him for a dancing competition
But no one will take me seriously.
And in the past week he hasn't turned up.
He might be overseas
And now he might be the greatest dancer of all time!

Lauren Russell (13)
Lodge School, Purley

Big Or Too Small?

Dear Mr Dragon,
Do you eat your babies?
I wonder what it's like when you get your sharp teeth,
Do you remember your first prey?
Do you remember your first prey?
Do you remember your first fiery breath?
I wonder what it's like being a dragon?

Dear Miss Mouse,
It's hard to speak,
It's sometimes hard with big animals
As I'm not a little ant,
Sometimes it's hard to say,
And sometimes it wants me to pick up a little nut,
But tell me what it's like to be small on stick legs.

Katie Hart (13)
Lodge School, Purley

The Unknown

It is a monster of supreme power,
It can be a gentile flower,
It has eyes as red as can be,
When they are seen, people do flee,
It also has eyes as blue as the sky,
Its wings stretch out, making it fly,
Its beastly legs cause earthquakes,
Buildings are destroyed and empty are the lakes,
Its quick feet allow it to sprint,
When it breathes there's a smell of mint,
From its nostrils comes a blazing light,
Even the volcanoes are given a fright,
As for the sun it feels a quiver,
Watching the nostrils create a river,
As for its teeth they're as hard as nails,
Back and forth goes its three tails,
This movement creates twisters,
Then they split and get sisters,
Then they will go and destroy a town,
Before chucking the debris right down,
Its nimble hands allow it to knit,
And upon one hand is a woolly mitt,
That's all that's known about the unknown.

Amir Mirza (12)
Merchant Taylors' School, Northwood

A White-Walled Prison

Me? What is there to know?
Burns, 3rd degree, to chest, arms and head.

I'm shackled to a moon-white bed,
People gaze at me, silent, as I prowl silently and oh so still,
Trapped in a red, scarred, torn cage;
Snow-coated jailers march down the aisle
Throwing glances at my fellow prisoners, swathed in cotton chains.

No key, no cure.
Even my voice is locked, sealed, forgotten,
The chemical-air stifles, making me cough and wheeze,
My skin sizzles and roasts,
The cool clear calm dripping into my tubes, useless.
The fire sentenced and imprisoned me, taking everything I had,

Dreams flash by: dashes through green,
Whole cream fingers intertwined with partners;
Never again.
Faded and smeared ghosts flicking in their peeling derelict dome -
Hiding places from shining scars and scared stares, true

But no one really escapes this prison.

Nicholas Tidmarsh (17)
Merchant Taylors' School, Northwood

Dust

Dust creeps through the air,
A handful of time that
Avoids the most frantic of clutches.
Pinned to your eyes by
A ray of light -

It
Falls,
Swirls,
Mingled with the breath
Of a god,
Of a mouse,
Of the world.

Propelled by a sigh
Like the clouds that skit through the sky
On a flat evening.

A handful of humanity,
Creeping through the air.

Alex Hill (18)
Merchant Taylors' School, Northwood

His Last Moments

He takes a breath; relishing the contractions of his lungs
His heart beats; a final attempt at satiating fingers, lips, tongues,

His pupils dilate; he never realised just how much there was to see
His muscles contract; exhausted flesh desperate to break free,

His teeth grind; a bitter taste settling deeply in his mouth
He shivers in the breeze; notices it's heading quickly south,

His palms sweat; reeking of his imminent fortune
And then he hears the voice; it carries an eerie, sickly croon,

A tear slides down his cheek; watery memories never forgotten
His lips turn blue; whispered pleas withering and rotten,

He releases a strangled sob; he doesn't want to go yet

There's a loud sound;
His mouth opens and he swallows a silver bullet.

Shanice Williams (17)
Merton College, Morden

Halloween Sun

Just over two decades since your soul burnt alive,
October baby, orange leaves never change.
Turn into winter, wither and wail,
And evolve through to summer.

A man to be admired by trusted pilgrims,
Liquid talent pouring through quick fingers
Onto loose strings. Pure, hollow wood,
Born to perform, cloud your body with ink.

Rich shadows cry out quietly from the stage side,
Adrenaline injection courses through you,
They are your minions, your components,
Your brothers, your friends.
Pump, faster, louder. And it's in your blood.

Aimi Walker (17)
Merton College, Morden

Bang, Boom!

It was day two in the trench, 4pm,
Then I heard it.
The guns, the Germans were here,
I panicked.
Bang! Boom!
Our men were dying,
I couldn't see to get ammunition.
Boom!
Our trench was blown up, I ran.
Someone shouted, 'Gas, gas, bomb!'
I found a gun,
Hm . . . that could be some fun.
I heard it again, 'Run, run!'
I jumped over a fence
Then a 250 Tiger tank came my way.
Boom! Boom!
No more fun.

Connor Hill (12)
Northolt High School, Northolt

The Black Starry Night

As I started to run through the black starry night
Every breath and every blink I made as if it was my last.
My knees went weak, memories rushing through my head,
Thinking of what would happen to my family if I was dead.
I hid by a bush and reloaded my gun,
Sped round the corner and all I could hear was, 'Run, run, run!'
I began to smile to hide my pain,
I could feel the blood rushing through my veins and out of my neck.
At least now I know what it is to feel pain.
Maybe I will start my journey again through the gates of Heaven.
Though I am gone, the body of a soldier
Will always know where it belongs.

Amy Dobson (12)
Northolt High School, Northolt

The Lost Poppies!

The lost poppies in the battlefield blowing in the wind,
They fight, they shout, they get blown away,
There's so much pain.

Lots of poppies died and left all alone,
They lose the things closest to home,
The love they have is blown away,
It's not like it comes back another day.

The brave poppies, dead and alone,
They're wishing that they could go home,
The blood drips down on the floor,
The pain has to travel to the family's door!

All the families in pain, wishing,
Just wishing to see the loved one's face.
They're just little poppies, lost and alone,
Waiting to go home! They're poor lost *souls!*

Laura Church (12)
Northolt High School, Northolt

World At War

I was starving to death in the trenches.
As I was reloading my gun, I was thinking
Of how I'd disappointed my mum,
How she didn't want me to be the endangered one.
I hoped and prayed that I would go home OK
But just then I saw a bullet coming my way.
So right then I heard my name, 'Run!' he yelled,
'Or you'll never see your family ever again!'
But I couldn't get away from the swift shooting bullet.
Black out.
So here I am, sleeping in my bed,
Wounded and shot in my arm and in my leg.

Mohamed Mohamed (12)
Northolt High School, Northolt

Judgement Day

As I hear the guns roar
Bloodstains on my window
People screaming, 'Help! Help!' for their lives
I am shaking,
My hair is sticking up

I am not sure what I am supposed to do

I can hear the footsteps of the Nazis coming to get me
Still I am not sure what I am supposed to do

I run up the stairs to grab some clothes
So I can run out of the pitch-black house
Still I am not sure what I am supposed to do

I hear the commander commanding the soldiers
To burn down every house
Still I am not sure what I am supposed to do . . .

Sharief Khalil (12)
Northolt High School, Northolt

Untitled

Bird, bird flying high as the sun rose in the sky
The eagle's colour shines so bright as it soars
Higher and higher in the sky
His beak as sharp as a blade
His claws pointed like dangerous daggers
The mountains are as white as snow
Trees as dark as night
As he flies through the trees into the darkness
His eyes shine like the stars
As he sees his prey he swoops and dives
Dinner is served.

Recardo Llewelyn (12)
Northolt High School, Northolt

Angels

If angels could be seen,
we would see faces that glow like the sun,
even during the day.
The wings as white as snow.
Smiles that fill you with joy.
Eyes of a natural colour,
but have the hint of heavenly light.
Their hair glossy and as light a feather.
Both male and female.
They stand behind us,
to protect and guide our inner souls,
but when our souls turn bad,
they might leave us.
I believe that they,
the angels, are the gods we believe in.
They let me believe and to make our own choice,
they will only guide us when the time comes.

Danielle Barclay (15)
Royal Alexandra & Albert School, Merstham

Is It Love?

The sight of a beautiful girl is one thing
Yet, for some reason it never hits you about her as a person.

She may be pretty as the wind dances in her hair with not a worry,
Inside though, she may be as ugly as mud.

Click, click, click, as her high heels hit the hard ground
Smiling slightly, as if she knows you're watching.

After days, weeks, maybe even months,
You pluck up the courage to talk to her face.

You're nervous, shy perhaps, trying to make an impression,
But when you get there, you think . . .

She's out of my league or it's too late now
But you don't listen to those thoughts, instead you ask her out.

Days go by with her by your side; you stick out like a sore thumb,
Soon those days turn into months, and you're drifting, drifting.

For a while you don't see her, as she's always with her mates,
Keeping away from her so-called boyfriend.

You think it's just a phase, her wanting some time to herself
But deep down you can feel there is something wrong.

You're tired of being on your own so you confront her,
Yet, she takes it the wrong way, and leaves you in your thoughts.

Somehow, something stays stuck between you, sticky stuff
And you feel it, a signal as strong as thunder.

You know she knows how you're feeling, but you keep to yourself,
Admiring her in your own time, in dreams with you still together.

In dreams you think, *nothing can stop us, we will be together always*
Then you look into her deep blue eyes and softly start to cry.

Scott Buckley (11)
Rydens School, Walton-on-Thames

Never Thought This Would Happen

A council estate was where I was born,
My life was always all old and torn,
As a job I wanted to go into music,
But was told I would never make it.

Always got into fights at school,
Made myself look like a fool,
I lived in a flat in a dodgy town,
And was told having dreams would just let me down.

I then got a job at a shop checkout,
But like everything else that didn't work out,
All I wanted to do was sing,
I wanted that more than anything.

I was still at school while this was going on,
And didn't care what happened, my heart felt dead and gone,
I got excluded at the end,
My life was turning round a bend.

One day when I lay in bed,
A sudden thought ran through my head,
Without thinking twice I got up to go,
I made my way over to my local music studio.

Soon I started singing on stage,
I always got people engaged,
They stopped and listened to me about my past,
They all agreed things should change, they were my own cast.

I am now a singer in a band,
My band mates listen, they give me a hand,
We tell people about poor areas, we work as a team,
So kids like me can have a dream.

Susanne Norris (12)
Rydens School, Walton-on-Thames

Depression

Depression chills your mind like a block of ice,
He glares at you, seeking his revenge,
He pounces like a tiger,
Darting through the night,
He grabs a knife and stabs you in the back,
With a big fright,

Pain and sadness flows into your blood,
He punches you in the jaw,
You scream and shriek,
While he seeks his next death,
You cry in pain,
Helpless and on your own,
He drags the dead people to his cove,
Underneath a gravestone to keep his secret unknown,
This only happens at night,
When people will yelp with fright.

What a wicked murderer he is,
He roasts people on a hot burning fire,
He boils like a huge volcano,
Exploding every second with harmful words and actions,
He fizzes and glares at everyone he meets.

Katie Stubbenhagen (11)
Rydens School, Walton-on-Thames

My Mother Teresa Poem

You make me happy when everything's wrong
You make me keep going when the road seems long
You make me laugh throughout my depression
You make happiness my new obsession.

When I'm looking at my kennel and there ain't no light
You are there, shining well bright
Suicide, I would never go near
For when I think of you I have nothing to fear.

Even though I met you when I was really young
And thank you for choosing to be a nun
You didn't turn me away for having a cleft lip
And when I would fall, you'd catch me if I would slip.

Thank you Mother Teresa, for looking after me when I was born
Otherwise no help, another death someone would mourn
I have a little picture of you and I look at it every single day
Just my way of saying I love you in every single way.

Karuna Whitehead (14)
Rydens School, Walton-on-Thames

The War With The Roses

The war with the Roses,
Why did this have to be?
I want us here together,
I want her here with me.

Before I left forever,
She gave something to me.
A bouquet of red roses,
So beautiful and pretty.

I'm going to miss you now,
I'll never be able to come back,
So goodbye my love, forever,
I'm going to the war, with the Roses.

Jacob Bennett (12)
St Paul's Catholic College, Sunbury-on-Thames

The Battlefield

On the battlefield,
There is uncontrollable pain.
Longing for escape,
From the suffering hell hole.
Bomb shells flutter,
From down below.

Blood flooding everywhere,
From sudden gunshots.
Piercing screams can be heard.
We want mercy.
But we can never give up!
Fighting for our lives.
Fighting for our freedom.

Anger and sadness;
Grieving for leaving home,
Children being forgotten,
Selfishness and killing,
How will we live
With these unforgiving sins?

Dragging dead to the ground;
Pretending they never lived,
As the dreaded gas comes in,
It drains and floods,
Lives of innocent ones.
People who don't deserve to die.

The land has been destroyed,
Graves have been filled.
Although many loved ones
Never got the chance
To say goodbye.
The poor soldiers never come home.

Mud encloses dead corpses.
Lucky ones say farewell;
People sing hand in hand.
Friendship grows again.

All is forgiven.

Aniqa Kaderbhai (11)
St Paul's Catholic College, Sunbury-on-Thames

War

Before the war, life was good,
We all had plenty of food.

Before the war had begun,
Everyone used to have more fun.

Before the war we played in the street,
Playing with a football at our feet.

Before the war happy faces could be found,
And a warm bed where you could sleep so sound.

Before the war we were free to roam,
And we were also safe in our own home.

During the war life had to change,
Always aware of the bullets' range.

During the war bombs would smash down,
Ripping apart our homes and our towns.

During the war life was so hard,
Managing with only a ration card.

During the war the world was not a good place,
Entire families gone without trace.

During the war it was six years of Hell,
But on August 14th 1945 we rang the victory bell.

After the war we had to rebuild our country so dear,
Living our lives once more without fear.

After the war many tears were cried.
By those whose loved ones had died.

After the war food was still hard to get,
No fish and chip suppers just yet.

After the war we had to right what went wrong,
Working hard to make our nation again, become strong.

After the war the pain's never gone,
For grieving families it lingers on and on . . .

Harry Dew (11)
St Paul's Catholic College, Sunbury-on-Thames

Love

Golden sun smashing on the blue sea,
Yellow sand blowing in the wind,
Two lovers leaving footprints,
Adoring each other,
Drawing love hearts on the yellow sun,
Sun beaming on the yellow sand,
Love.
Holding hands,
Swinging hands,
Running to each other,
Her long, brown hair in the sun,
His blue eyes shining out brightly,
Love.
Wearing dresses,
Wearing shorts,
Summer's hot sun,
Summer's forever,
Together forever,
Love.
He goes, leaves her behind,
She cries,
Wet tears rolling down her face,
He fights thinking of,
His love,
She thinks about him,
Every second of the day,
Love.
He returns,
She runs to his arms,
My love, I'm back!
Love.

Ana Correia (11)
St Paul's Catholic College, Sunbury-on-Thames

Love In Contrast To War

The rain patters down from God's heavenly kingdom
A female ghost protected by the queen herself sits on
A lone egg, *crack! Crack!*
New life emerges from within, its body as grey as the clouds
themselves.

War! War! War has been declared, people sit trembling guarding
what they have.
Boom! Crash! The first bombs launched from Hell, hit.
New fear, as dark as the Devil himself.

Its new independent wings shimmer in the moonlight
Transformed by a miracle, its once grey, shining feathers
Are now white forgiven ones.
The surreal, magical mist engulfed its legendary body.

'We're winning lads! It's a miracle!' Can be heard over
The mind-blowing racket. The army trudges forward,
Uplifted, guns a blazing.

The mature swan glides to its permanent love.
They come together, merging into a heart shape.
Gazing into each others eyes; the heart floats downstream.
Both oblivious to the future . . .

The lone swan mourns, staring at its pure, white double
Her partner is dead and the devilish, dark clouds return . . .
There is no more love in her empty heart.
Her body shrinks slowly into the infinite distance.

A lone soldier stares at the destroyed, derelict buildings.
His friends lay, limp on the ground.
Tears stream, awkwardly down his face, whilst he murmurs,
'Why, why . . .'

Daniel Grimwade (12)
St Paul's Catholic College, Sunbury-on-Thames

War

The battlefield is as silent as thee,
Just a long silence with no merciful plea.
The odour of death lingers around,
With so many dead bodies and more to be found,
The terror of murder screams in your head,
Of that fateful person who is now dead.

The horror of murder turns you insane,
Turns you from person to person in vain,
The thought never leaves wherever you go,
From the uneasy feeling of killing the foe.
The man always haunts you even at day,
For you took a life which you can't repay.
As you just sit there thinking fast,
You think even deeper into your past.

As the sergeant says to go over the top,
You realise this time you're in for the chop,
It's kill or be killed,
As your quest is fulfilled.
As you climb over the bullet hits you,
Only knowing your friends are hit too,
As you lie there dying slow,
You realise now it's time to go.
As of the day the proven lure,
Had caught you out and took you to war.

Ben Lyons (11)
St Paul's Catholic College, Sunbury-on-Thames

My Friend My Love My Everything

My friend, my love my everything
I give my life for you but there's one thing I must know
Do you love me too?
Your eyes shine like the stars a million miles away
I would go to the moon just to hear you say.

My friend, my love my everything
I want you here with me
To see the beauty of the sunset on the beach.

My friend, my love my everything
I cry more each day
And every time the wind blows by I hear it call your name.
War is such a brutal thing you can't believe your eyes.
Every time you step outside someone dies.

My friend, my love my everything
Please hear me say
I want you to remember me every day.
I love you more
I'll be back to you
Soon, my shining little star.

My friend, my love my everything
Is who you are!
My friend, my love
My everything.

Natalie Marie McGrail (11)
St Paul's Catholic College, Sunbury-on-Thames

Memory

As I grow old I look back
Remembering my only romance

Walking along a beach on a summer's evening
Watching the sunset go down
And then he broke it to me:
He was going to war.

I said-no

He said-don't worry, it'll be fine!

A month later he went to war.
Due home in six months.
Five long months I waited
Reading his letters from the trenches . . .
Until one day
A letter came-not from him.

His officer told me he was dead
Killed with seven other comrades by a shell,
German shell exploded over the parapet.

Now, walking along the beach
I look at the seashells in his memory
As if he never died
His spirit is always with me.

Jessica-Louise Mansell (12)
St Paul's Catholic College, Sunbury-on-Thames

What Is War?

We see the bullets hit the floor
We don't know what to do but run out the door.
My face is dried up with tears of shame
Wondering what it would be like to have all the fame.
We know it's the end but can't bear anymore.
We have to face the facts now
That's just war.

Nora Bakoa-Kela (11)
St Paul's Catholic College, Sunbury-on-Thames

The Last Day

Bang, bang, bang!
Was all I could hear as I kissed my lady goodbye,
The kiss lasted for such a long time,
Lots of things were running through my mind;
Will I ever see her again?
Will I even survive this terrible war?
Will I see my family?
As I got further away from the coast,
Her beautiful face was getting smaller and smaller
And a cold salty tear dribbled down my sore cheek.

As soon as we arrived at Normandy, a shiver shivered down my spine.
I jumped out the boat and swam to shore.
Those thoughts were still running through my mind,
The first thing I could hear was . . . *bang*! and, 'C'mon guys!'
I could see the enemy getting closer and I said, 'This is it.'
My commander shouted, 'Fire!'
That hurtful sound of gunshots
And the smell of gunpowder was revolting.
I saw the German who was about 300m away from me.
He shot his gun and I watched the bullet speed towards me
And *blank* . . .

Jacob Matthew Walters (13)
St Paul's Catholic College, Sunbury-on-Thames

World At War!

War!
Soldiers,
Troops all lined up,
Ready for battle.
Killing, stabbing,
All day long,
Non-stop,
Dead!

Brian Ontola (12)
St Paul's Catholic College, Sunbury-on-Thames

Love

The glistening reflection of the bright orange sun
Love, affection and adoration
A gleaming smile
Such a pretty sight
The cherishable memories
The faithfulness shown in them
The devotion

The passion
The optimism shown
For all to see
All the flirting
Equals
A big happy family
The charm they show
Is a sight to see

Each other's Valentine

Meant to be on a beach
The waves at their feet
Worshipping their devotion
They were meant to be
They were meant to be.

Kieran Baker (12)
St Paul's Catholic College, Sunbury-on-Thames

Love And War

I cannot compare thee to a summer's day,
You are so beautiful in every way.
I will go to war for thou love will never end,
If I die do remember me and our love,
I will fight for love no matter what it takes,
We will go to the stars one day but for now,
Goodbye.

Abel Tesfagabar (12)
St Paul's Catholic College, Sunbury-on-Thames

Family/Love/War

Love, love is a white dove sent from above.
I come to Earth to conquer fear.
I come to Earth to say oh dear.

I see children are dying,
Bombs are flying and people are crying.

My family is scared,
Our pet died but we still cared.

We love each other through good and bad,
It's hard to keep a smiling face when you're so sad.

What's going on with the world,
I was watching the news this morning when the soldier hurled.

I love my life and family deep down,
Although it's hard these days not to keep on a frown.

We have fun sometimes
Especially when we have competitions busting rhymes.

Love, love is a white dove sent from above.

I came to Earth to conquer fear,
I came to Earth to say oh dear.

Suheila Moreira (12)
St Paul's Catholic College, Sunbury-on-Thames

Love Is Special

Love is a beautiful thing,
It is like a bird's song in the morning,
Love is like a summer's day,
Love is like a blue sky,
Love is happiness,
Love is about friendship,
Your loved ones are special,
Look after them till the day you die,
There is only one special person for me and you.

Emilia Ashworth (12)
St Paul's Catholic College, Sunbury-on-Thames

War And Love

Love
Love and family
Love with friends
Love with God and everyone.
What is love?
Ask this family they will tell you
To adore someone
And love someone with passion
Loving isn't just romance
It's also caring for other people
War.
Black, grey, red those are the
Colours of war
A soldier said.
Black for anger, grey for sadness
And for the whole place, red for blood.
Those are the colours associated
With war.
War is pure anger and
Upsets near enough
Everyone.

Mateusz Chocianoaski (12)
St Paul's Catholic College, Sunbury-on-Thames

Untitled

Love
Peaceful
Beautiful
Love forever
Flowers all around
Changing your life
Wonderful
This is
Love.

Juwon Ogunbodede (11)
St Paul's Catholic College, Sunbury-on-Thames

Family Is The Love!

Who can give
Love and care
Happiness and support?
Only family can give you love
Family is the love!

Scared and worried
Sad and lonely
Only family can help you
Family is the love.

Who can give you more than this?
Every day with you
Every day caring for you
What do you want more than this?
Family is the love.

Family is the love
Family is the love!
That is the biggest love you can ever receive
Family is the love.

Alexiya Plammoottil (12)
St Paul's Catholic College, Sunbury-on-Thames

War Is Upon Everyone!

People are dying
As birds are flying,
Giving messages to each other,
But they were shot, what a bother.
Bombs were shot in all directions,
As I looked at my reflection.
Blood was falling down my cheek,
I became weak,
As I looked in the sky,
Warships fly,
Death is upon everyone.

Frances Gerner (11)
St Paul's Catholic College, Sunbury-on-Thames

Goodbye

I cannot say goodbye, not this time,
My arms clench around you they don't want
To let go, my heart pounding, tears
Running down my face, don't leave, not yet.
As I look in to your weary eyes
I can see that your heart is breaking, but you
Contain your emotion. As the cold
Sea drifts upon my feet, my stomach tightens
Like an iron fist and my tears I cannot
Control. My eyes widen and my heart is racing
As the dreaded time draws near.
I hear guns and cries for help but you are all I
Imagine. Faith is what I need and is
What I will get, the time has come,
I imagine your blood, sweat and tears.
Your cries for help haunt me, but I can only
Live in hope that we meet again.
So for now my love, I must bid you adieu.
Goodbye!

Miranda Hurley (13)
St Paul's Catholic College, Sunbury-on-Thames

Untitled

Why does war happen?
It's stupid, so many troops lose their lives
As they go to battle.
Why do we do it?
It's not very clever.
In the end what have we learnt?
Killing people for what,
Standing up for their rights?
In the end, no light down the tunnel.
Stop before we kill a whole nation.

Johnson Chandigere (12)
St Paul's Catholic College, Sunbury-on-Thames

Untitled

I look in the sky
A big flash of light
Changes colour
Blue to red
I look around me,
Friends and foes
Tired or dead
I sit down exhausted
And cough because of
The thick smoke all around me
Loved ones at home,
Drained from tears
They hope I'm alive
My mind I think for
A second or two and
Say to myself is it over
Have we won the smell
Of smoke and death takes
Me in total darkness.

Daniel Joseph Lawrence (11)
St Paul's Catholic College, Sunbury-on-Thames

The Poem Of Goodness

Roses are red
Violets are blue
There is love in the air
People going away
The hatred in the air
People crying and dying
Love is everywhere.

Kalvin Matharu (12)
St Paul's Catholic College, Sunbury-on-Thames

War Equals Nothing

Why does war go on?
It is just another disaster waiting to happen
The fear of the soldiers
Lingers through the wilderness
As well as the troughs
And the fear of us
We wish for peace from day to day
But there are many lives
We can never repay
And when all the money
Is going to waste
Some lay on nothing, they are hurt and in pain
More troops have been sent on a big, long journey
Their families hope that
They return in harmony
When the war ends
And it's time to say goodbye
Their relatives sit there and start to cry.

Thang Nguyen (11)
St Paul's Catholic College, Sunbury-on-Thames

A Great Thing Called Love

But no other name smells so sweet,
By walking backward they shall meet,
They take photos to show affection,
Then bump into each other with perfection.

Thou family est just begun,
The woman becomes a mum,
Then they have a little lad,
While the man is still a dad.

Then at night they say, 'I love you!'
Then they say, 'Get to bed you!'
Sometimes love is so unpredictable,
But like a table, it's so mendable.

Love, love, love, such a beautiful thing,
It makes yourself ting,

Now every poem must have an end,
But this one is just going to bed.

Hayley-Leanne Headland (12)
St Paul's Catholic College, Sunbury-on-Thames

Where Is The Love?

The world is at war killing little ones, silenty
But deadly, smelly and chemical gasses killing everyone.

So, why don't you ask yourself, where is the love?
Where is the love? The love, the love of God?

We were made by God in under a day to be happy,
not heartbroken, so where is the love?

He made the beautiful world, the sparkling sky
all of space but why?

He did this for us to show he really cares,
He made man, he made woman
not to have affairs but to be generous, kind and loving.

Luke Bowyer (12)
St Paul's Catholic College, Sunbury-on-Thames

My Dear Sweetheart

I know that you are safe somewhere,
With someone you can trust,
I need to see your smiling face,
Your golden locks, I must!

I sense your rosy presence,
My heart it longs to beat,
When I get home to see you,
On the corner, we shall meet.

And once I leave this awful place,
And see the golden leaves,
I know that I'll be safe again,
And you are all I need.

The flowers now are blooming,
And I am reassured,
For when I'm finally home again,
My heart, it will be cured.

Alicia Willoughby (12)
St Paul's Catholic College, Sunbury-on-Thames

War Is Over

The proud leader stands on top of the hill with his secretary,
Looking down to all the people.
Their hearts racing as fast as they can -
Beat, beat, beat just like a drum.
Dead bodies lie on the ground,
Drowned in blood, some still have their shotguns in their hands.
Suddenly, the bright yellow sun comes out from behind the dark, gloomy clouds.
Trees start to grow green leaves, flowers start to blossom and birds start to sing.
Nature dances around in the gentle breeze.
Everything comes to life when war is over!

Jade Cook (12)
St Paul's Catholic College, Sunbury-on-Thames

War

War is a chaotic battle.
Thousands of men fight for country but not all survive.
People are upset if they have lost their loved ones and will be very sad.
If you are one of the survivors then you are sad because
you have lost your friends but be happy because you survived.
You can die by gas, bombs, ships, guns, tanks and planes.
If your country loses or if the war carries on for many
years then you are devastated.
As prolonged war brings lots of unhappiness as many people are
getting injured or dying, bringing a lot of sorrow to the country.
You should get a medal like Johnson Beharry because he is
Protecting his country, family and friends and they will be proud of you.
Knowing you are a good soldier.
But always remember war is a fierce battle and one
Should always be brave enough to fight it.

André Hanson (11)
St Paul's Catholic College, Sunbury-on-Thames

The Fighting Goes On

War and hatred in the air,
Care and love are nowhere,
Why can't we all just be at peace?
But no, the fighting goes on.

Gunshots, shouting and explosions around me,
Tears and cries of frightened men,
All wishing that they could flee,
And be home with their family.
But no, the fighting goes on.

Pity and sorrow for those who died,
They fought for their country and really tried,
You would think that when one war ends, lessons would be learned,
But no, another war starts and the fighting goes on . . .

Stephanie Brown (12)
St Paul's Catholic College, Sunbury-on-Thames

The Four Seasons

Autumn fire
Apples falling from a tree, hoping not to go rotten.
The old silver birch looks snowy,
The bark is silver and dying leaves almost white.
The sun is bright yet the air leaves me shivering.
I see children in hats, coats and scarves playing with shiny brown conkers

The trees are full of red, orange and yellow, a beautiful fire
The flames that float on the pond are little burning boats.
The wind blows the embers around the sky like birds.

Dead sea (winter)
Last week the park was full of beauty, full of red, orange and yellow,
But now fire has turned to dirt, the wind blows it past my feet like the tide
The apples that fell were never gathered and drowned in a sea of brown.

The brown sea has covered the flowers; the cold has scared away the animals.
The scent of bluebells has changed to rotting leaves
The pond is grey and lifeless, little flaming boats have turned to ash.
The clouds mask the sun from sight, turning pale blue to a dull grey.
And if it were to be night you would not know the stars still shine.

Spring
The park is full of apple blossom, the petals in the pond are pink boats
Even though the sky is cloudy
And it's been raining it is definitely getting warmer.
I am no longer waking up in darkness
And when I get home the sun is still up
The strong wind blows the scent of bluebells;
I can smell them from the other side of the park
The trees are full of leaves and birds sing from the highest branches

The dull green grass is now rich and vibrant,
Covered in daisies and buttercups
Little grey ducklings skim the top of the water
And by summer they will be beautiful white swans
If you look closer you can see gold,
Like jewels just out of reach, little glittering fish below the water.

Summer
The heat makes me feel sleepy; I could lie on this bench forever
The taste of strawberries is still in my mouth
I'm all alone but surrounded by nature
The ugly ducklings have transformed into big, beautiful, white swans
But geese never stop squawking, not even to take breath,
Still it's nicer than a lifeless pond
The cherry sunsets are enchanting,
Changing white marshmallow clouds to pink candyfloss
And the flowers sink into a slumber in the darkening vermilion tint.

Harriet Armatage (16)
Stowford College, Sutton

Ode To A Flamingo

Female flamingo writes a love poem to her love

Oh my lovely pink flamingo
How I wish you spoke the lingo
Oh how your strong legs stand
In the water as you land
With you by my side
Forever we can glide.

Male flamingo writes a love poem to his love

You're as fluffy as pink candyfloss
Your eyes shining with gloss
I love the way you flutter your wing
And how I love to hear you sing
Nothing will pull us apart
You will always be in my heart.

Danica Markovic (13)
The Green School, Isleworth

Sunflower

A sunflower delicately weak and small,
Wishes to be powerful, strong and tall,
So that he can see over the brick wall.

Although there are many sights to see,
There will never be anything as beautifully,
As what he saw before this catastrophe.

There is only the wind and soil to comfort him,
As he stands in the dawn, middle and dim,
Waiting to be as tall as Tim!

He towers tall day and night,
Oh what a wonderful sight,
Not for me - I desire his height.

He can see over the brick wall,
Not for me I have to haul,
But someday - I will be tall.

A month has passed and still no luck,
I haven't grown, I think I'm stuck,
Why me who's in this muck?

The sunflower weeps every day,
Among the wind and breeze he sways,
There he lies and there he stays.

A shout of joy, a pierce of glee!
Sunflower screams abruptly!
He has reached his final destiny!

The tallest sunflower in the land,
Emotions of proudness as he stands,
He is not and no longer will be bland.

Just one peek and only glance,
He had only one chance,
Triumph fulfils him and he begins to dance . . .

Amber Osgood (14)
The Green School, Isleworth

Apple's Juice

Apple juice
It's not an apple
Nor a juice
It's an amazing combination of them two.

It's the juice from the apple
Taken out ever so delicately that it's hard to get right.
Robots squeeze it.
They work all day
And all night
But these days
They don't do it right.

They squeeze it too hardly
In the year 2020
Only humans could do it lightly
In the year 2010.

I have built a time machine
To go back to 2010
I have to see the green
Get away from 2020.

I drink the juice in 2010
It's like Heaven now and then.
Feeling the sweetness and sourness going down my throat
I think I'll stay here forever
I'll live in a boat but I can't, I must go back.

I say goodbye to the apple farmer,
Who falls asleep wishing he could get warmer,
He mumbles in his sleep,
'I wish that boy stayed in 2010.
He could have seen himself be born.
I'm the grandfather of that boy called Ben.'

Amara Hameed (13)
The Green School, Isleworth

My Fateful Journey

I bore the bodies of a nation's sorrow,
I carried them forward into tomorrow,
A tomorrow the President will never see.
The soul of his wife died inside of me
In November 1963.
The sun was shining, sparkling down
Upon the crowd, waving and smiling, in that town.
I carved a line, so broad and straight,
Along that road, but there was hate.
. . . It lay in wait.

Hiding in the crowd, unknown to me,
The motorbike riders and security,
The gunman took JFK in his sight,
Pulled the trigger, day turned to night.
Despair replaced my light.
The single shot rang out, straight, true,
Like lightning, it forced itself through
Flesh and bone,
It had found its home . . . the crack of sound,
Spread wide, around
. . . People fell to the ground.

I feel such shame,
I was to blame,
They all looked at me,
Their eyes could see
But not believe
That I could leave
. . . Him, unguarded.

Time slowed right down, they looked around
In disbelief, in grief.

Laura Baker (13)
The Green School, Isleworth

Five Signs For A Summery Spring

Sign one
The bright yellow sun,
Hanging in the sky,
Brightening everyone's day,
With his warm golden rays,
Beaming a smile at us on earth.

Sign two
Flowers like fairies,
Twirling their dance in the breeze,
With their colourful coats,
And sweet fragrance smell,
It's true, each one unique like you and me.

Sign three
The green grass,
Prickly and long,
Chatting to each one's neighbour
Their big friendship song.

Sign four
Hear the spectacular birds,
Humming their wonderful tune,
Tweet, tweet, tweeting,
All day long,
In such an amazing way.

Sign five
Taste the wonderful,
Summery spring air,
What a breeze,
Full of love and care,
Five signs for a summery spring.

Syeda Hussain (12)
The Green School, Isleworth

Maple

Free as a bird
Locked in four walls,
Not seen or heard
As I shriek my silent call

Yet nobody can see
That I am perfectly stable,
As long as I am free
Alongside my Maple

They say it's tough for me
They say I can't cope,
Yet I beg and I plea
And promise not to tighten the rope

Mother says she's cheerful,
And safe in God's love,
But I know she is fearful,
Even though she's up above

I have to protect
And give her my hand
I can lend this effect
If I desert this land

Bright brown eyes
And striking red hair
Lit up the sky
And made you stare

Then the disease came
And made her unstable
Out went the candle flame
And so did my beautiful Maple.

Sabrina Sahota (13)
The Green School, Isleworth

If I Was A Head Teacher

If I was a head teacher,
There'd be no lessons, not even one,
Because all lessons are boring,
And we'd be too busy having fun.

If I was a head teacher,
There would be school trips every day,
We'd all go to Walt Disney,
And we wouldn't have to pay.

If I was a head teacher,
No one would get told off,
You would never get detentions,
You'd miss a month's school for a cough.

If I was a head teacher,
You could bring in any pets,
There would be no bullies,
And no one making threats.

If I was a head teacher,
I'd give everyone a camera pen,
You could go on the computers all day long
And chat on MSN.

If I was a head teachor,
You could turn up when you like,
You could play outside all day,
And go on your bike.

But no one would learn anything,
No one would be smart,
Maybe we should do some lessons,
But just a few to start.

Gabriella Heuchan (12)
The Green School, Isleworth

Stand!

As I walk through the streets of London
I hear people cry
I hear people screaming
I see people die

As I walk through the streets of London
I see the upper class
I see their fur coats
And shoes made of glass

As I walk through the streets of London
I hear sirens call
I see police run in
To a crowded shopping mall

As I walk through the streets of London
I gasp as I see
A knife slicing into an innocent young lady

As I walk through the streets of London
I fall to a halt
As I hear a gunshot fire
I see the blood drench my back

But then in that street in London
I hear a voice in my ear
It's gentle and soft
And ever so dear
Even though I'm in pain
I can swear it's a man
And he is simply saying
'My child
Stand!'

Kiyana Lewis (14)
The Green School, Isleworth

Lonely

Loneliness, happy or sad?
A mixed emotion.
Is this so bad?
To sit alone,
No one there.
To sit alone,
Without a care.

Loneliness. Is it such a bad thing?
Lost in a world.
No cares to bring.
To sit alone,
No one there with you.
To sit alone,
No one to compare you to.

Loneliness. But is it really fair?
Lost in a world.
No one that cares.
To sit alone,
No one there.
To sit alone,
Is it fair?

Loneliness. Both happy and sad.
A mixed emotion,
That's not so bad.
To sit alone,
Without a clue.
But never alone,
Loneliness there with you . . .

Jelena Vukovic (14)
The Green School, Isleworth

Nowhere To Run

My life is shattered,
It has no hope,
In a shelter
Hidden by a gritted slope.

Planes fly over,
Big bombs come down,
Big explosion,
In war victory will frown.

Broken homes,
Broken lives,
Broken families,
I have to survive.

The shelter is bombed,
My life is at risk,
I run,
I hide,
My heart beats like birds' wings,
I stop.
Time stops.
Life stops.
Silence . . .

I'm lost,
Not free,
I'm captured,
The end of me,
Life stops.
Silence.

Claudia Chappell (13)
The Green School, Isleworth

1914 - Sacrifice For Glory - 1918

World War One not World War Two, yes World War One I say,
A horrible, scary and frightening time which is still remembered today,
Hidden in the trenches all day long, keeping my head down low,
Sand and grit are thrown in your eyes from bombs that forever explode,
Running in lines, rifles in hands,
Sacrificing ourselves to save our comrades.

Bang, bang, bang! go the bullets from the guns,
Now no turning back now, so just run, run, run,
Everyone's shouting and screaming from place to place,
All the guns that are mine are my friends',
My comrades won't die if they're always in my hands.

My big bold helmet protecting my head,
Just another day of war with the sun up ahead,
The sun is like a big yellow ball,
Cuddling us, to keep us all warm,
The ground is like a sinking sea,
Every step you take your feet can't see.

The last shot is taken, the war is finally won,
You turn to see a smiling man pointing at you with his gun,
He pulls the trigger, your eyes go puffy and fall down to your knees,
You think to yourself, I don't want to die now so someone help me please,
You relax your head and close your eyes 'cause the pain is finally gone,
You're going to the heavens above because your life is now done.

Lauren Boyce (12)
The Green School, Isleworth

The Game Of Life And Death

The ship and sea play a game
They play it all the time
Then after a while the ship thought
A new tactic it had to find.
It rolled a six, it played its ace
And gambled many a life.

The ship it changed its piece
To a steamship called the Titanic
They called her 'unsinkable'
As 16 water-tight compartments she had
The sea just chose, the Atlantic Ocean
And put icebergs in the path.

The Titanic left from Southampton
As confident as a peacock in a zoo
But it floundered when it hit ice
There was nothing it could do
As the people entered the water
Shouts and shrieks pierced the air
Screams, screams that gradually died out
As the coldness was too much to bear.

And this is how the sea claimed its prize
When only 700 were left alive
And it showed the world that still
It is capable to kill
The sea it won
The ship it lost
And 1,500 people were the cost.

Catrin Beetham (13)
The Green School, Isleworth

Paradise Island

The cacophonous caw of a parrot,
As it swoops through lush green trees,
Crystal clear turquoise waters,
That cool hot and clammy skin,
This is my paradise island.

A thud, clatter noise when
Across golden sands a coconut tumbles from its lofty perch,
Its oozy milk runs like fingers
Escaping into the waves that caress the shore,
This is my paradise island.

Upon the horizon an army of sentry-like trees,
That stretch and pierce the skies,
They whisper secrets to their ally, the wind
And it takes them far away,
This is my paradise island.

The harmonious sound of a dancing waterfall,
Heavenly flavoured fruits,
Tantalising my taste buds,
Soft, white sand trickling through my toes,
This is my paradise island.

Explosions of sound,
Glorious sights,
Velvety tastes,
Everything is cloaked in beauty,
This is my paradise island.

Georgina Smith (12)
The Green School, Isleworth

The Life Of A Raindrop (The Liquid Of Life)

It was crowded and busy and stuffy,
It was getting too heavy, too dark, too sad.

So I sacrificed myself.

Drip-dropping, down,
Lower, lower and lower still.
Tracing the outline of my feelings.
An indefinite colour. An indefinite shape.
I saw the others,
They twirled like ballerinas on a fully lighted stage.
They saw me and muttered:
'Water is the liquid of life, and we are this liquid.'
Their words cradled me like a mother clutching her baby.
I am indestructible! I am invincible! I am the one!

I woke up in a damp ditch,
Not in the best of all moods.
My heart raced, there was an odd figure standing in my shadow,
It was looking straight at me.
It trotted over determinedly and bowed its head,
Like it was worshipping me.
I found myself laughing, it was tickling me,
Something red, dry and unpleasant had confronted me.
I was disappearing, and fast,
Like a chocolate pudding in a hungry person's bowl.

I started to realise what was happening,
Have I become a lifesaver?

Eleanor Franks (11)
The Green School, Isleworth

Men On The Moon

Men in helmets,
Men in suits,
What a strange sight it must be on the moon.
Floating heads,
Floating bodies,
Floating around the strange sight, the moon.

Flashes flashed,
Buttons pressed,
Pictures taken to be sent back to Earth.
The victory happened,
We shall now make our mark,
Pierce the rock with the American flag.

Dancing it dances,
Without a care in the world,
Like Darcey Bussell on that dancing show,
We've done it, we've done it, we've done it again,
We're first to have found something
As amazing as the moon.

Through the victory, it went unnoticed,
That it was dark, mysterious, cold and strange.
The land was barren yet it felt full.
A vast emptiness, no sound to be heard,
The atmosphere on the moon,
We have found it
And are proud to be the men on the moon.

Kateryna Cutler (13)
The Green School, Isleworth

The Beautiful Waves

Sitting silently, breathing in and out, sitting silently
Rippling across the tranquil ocean
Suddenly a tremble grew below me like a boat starting up
Sending ripples that pushed us all back with its powerful engine
All of a sudden I was quivering, trembling with the ocean.

I felt myself grow taller, tougher, violent and vicious
I grew so that I now towered over the stunning bay that stood before me
Whilst admiring its beauty, I did not notice how the tide was pulling me in with it
Sucking me in, hissing at me
Tourists were gathering like a flock of birds being fed.

High-pitched, piercing screams began to break out
I collapsed on the land, snaking my way through streets, houses, hotels
People were struggling to survive
Clinging onto bars, I was carrying dead bodies
Brothers, sisters, mums, dads, grandmas and grandads
Just like rubbish.

They were petrified, I slowly breathed in
Sucking all the water back in stranding people at sea
Some dead, some paralysed, dead and dying
I'd destroyed these people's lives now they'd never be the same
But yet did they know I'd strike again
Destroying their lives for all.

Jessica Forsyth (12)
The Green School, Isleworth

My Goldfish

Once I had a goldfish
Who was so bold,
His fins were bright gold,
I really loved my goldfish.

My goldfish's eyes were blue,
Like the sky in the air,
So many people loved him,
As he had no hair.

He was the best pet I've ever had,
He was at all not bad,
That pet was my first pet,
He was always on a bet.

He was the pet in the starlight,
He was really so bright,
He did many different tricks,
He even balanced bricks.

He did really cool juggling,
He got everybody bubbling,
His tricks were so funny,
It was even better than a bunny.

But one day my goldfish became ill,
So he couldn't pay his bill,
He balanced too many bricks,
So he couldn't do his tricks.

Michal Abraham (12)
The Green School, Isleworth

The Vulture Who Glared

The vulture who glared
Sat and stared
At the child who fell so hungry and weak
Defeated by famine he yelled and screeched
As the vulture who glared with vicious, hungry eyes
Stared at the boy until he died

Tweet, tweet, tweeted the bird
As weak as he was well that's what he heard
He knew he was the next prey in line
It had now come, it was his time
He then slipped away like a cold winter's day
There he lay and there he would stay

Oh, how the vulture adored this sight
He stumbled to the boy before it was night
Finally he had something to eat
Something he longed for in such hazy heat
He couldn't eat him, he was too thin
All he had were bones and skin

The vulture who glared
Sat and stared
At the boy who lay there no more
Don't worry for the bird, he had more to explore
As the feathered bird left with his back held straight
He found someone else to stare at my mate . . .

Ourida Sichaib (13)
The Green School, Isleworth

Snow

Snow is like a white feather falling among the white river on the floor.
Snow is like a polar bear racing against the sky.
Snow is like a duvet draped around the Earth.
Snow is like a flock of white butterflies looking for cabbage
And coconut on chocolate cake fields.

Hodman Hussein (12)
The Green School, Isleworth

Monkey

Oh my mischievous monkey,
When you dance you are so funky,
The way you wiggle and jiggle,
It makes me want to giggle,
The way you swing in trees up high,
It's almost as if you fly.

Your friends I see are just the same,
It's almost if it's one big game,
To see who can annoy me the most,
Then they will go ahead and boast,
You try to annoy them instead,
But then comes in the head.

You run around so fast,
But in a race you're always last,
There's no need to cry,
I know that you always try,
To do your best,
Even though you're a little pest.

When we get back home,
I'm always on my phone,
Calling my friend,
Which drives you round the bend,
You always annoy our mother
Because you are my little brother!

Kate Richards (12)
The Green School, Isleworth

The Biggest Ship In The World

'The biggest ship in the world,'
They'll say,
As I pushed towards America,
The swaying, slashing sea,
Completely and utterly harmless to me.

'The biggest ship in the world,'
They'll say,
The children sang happily,
Every high-pitched perfect note,
Totally safe on the unsinkable boat.

'The biggest ship in the world,'
They'll say,
But the iceberg was impenetrable,
It was stronger than me,
So the ocean rushed in,
Through the gouged holes,
Guilty I felt, for all those wasted souls.

Sinking, sinking like a harpooned whale,
Hitting the bottom hard.
There I lay,
And there I'll stay,
Never forgotten on the seabed,
'The biggest ship in the world,'
They said.

Elizabeth Adcock (13)
The Green School, Isleworth

The Man Who Shook Hands With The Flag

I was the man who shook hands with the flag
Proud, proud I was
I had finally fulfilled my lifetime goal
Standing there, that day,
With my family made me smile,
As their teeth gleamed with pride,
I was the man who shook hands with the flag.

I was the king,
And the media were my ants,
Ants they were,
The media were my ants,
We would be like a tree of liberty,
I was the man who shook hands with the flag.

Famous I would be,
Followed by the media and looked upon by the whole of America,
I am the caretaker,
The keeper of the keys for all the states,
I was the man who shook hands with tho flag.

Just another day in my life,
But a day I will write about.
Standing there, that day,
Made me proud,
I was the man who shook hands with the flag!

Shalini Gupta (12)
The Green School, Isleworth

The Man Who Was Never There . . .

I was the man who was never there,
The man taking the pictures,
The man who never got a stare,
I was the second and never the first,
And nobody would really care.

I was the man who was never there,
The man capturing the footprints,
Whose pictures would make history everywhere,
Neil was the hero,
And it was not fair.

I was the man who was never there,
The man who was second on the mighty moon,
The flag blew in the light night breeze,
Like the waves rippling in the big blue sea,
The flag smiled, as it waved hello,
But I was not there, I would never know.

I was the man who was never there,
The second on the moon,
Who never got a stare,
I was the after party no one ever went to,
Yes I was the man who was never there,
'Cause I was the camera man who never got a stare.

Melissa Marsden (12)
The Green School, Isleworth

The River Thames

The river Thames is an orphan girl
Twisting and turning
Each day closer, but never close enough
Forever searching for a home
A teardrop runs down her cheek
She sighs
Will she ever find one?

Annabelle Wellington (13)
The Green School, Isleworth

I Enter In, I Enter Out

I enter the deep blue crystal sea
I call out to my companions
They answer back with their high-pitched voices

I see the bubbles
They are thoughts of pleasure
Trapped so they can never leave

I see them coming
The elegant fin
Swiftly coming towards me

She was greeting me
I got closer and closer
I put my leg slightly over her
Then we zoomed through the refreshing water

But now it's my time
My time to go
I am mortal you see

But I'll be back
Don't know how
Don't know when
But I will
I know I will.

Deekshika Preman (12)
The Green School, Isleworth

Listen To Your Heart

Look around,
Stop and stare.
Listen closely,
He says he cares.
Don't start crying,
Don't start to laugh.
Lean right in
And listen to your heart.
Start to smile,
Start to care.
He's right in front of you,
He's always there.
You're not alone,
Just jump back in.
Listen to your heart,
It's not a sin.

You can taste the sweetness of your tears,
You can see everything without any fears.

Just listen to your heart,
Everything is new.
Smile at him,
He's in love with you.

Nehal Canji (12)
The Green School, Isleworth

The Pink Rose

The rose twirled on her stem
As she put pink lipstick on her friend
She let down her flowery pink hair
She was the most beautiful rose but nobody cared
Her skin was gentle, her skin was soft
But she dusted all her petals off
She let out a sweet smell
She was like a cute golden bell.

Aaliyah Douglin (11)
The Green School, Isleworth

Blue Dreams

The water dripped into the sea
Spreading out at the bottom
It separates into two parts
Into two beautiful oceans

I walked along the ground
My bare feet on the soft grass
Walking along the path to joy
It gets wetter at every step

I stand on the peck of a hill
Looking up and down at the clear blue
I feel the sweet smelling air
And the wet water on my feet

Seeking the sky so blue
With fluffy clouds everywhere
I fell back on the soft green
Thinking about the happy memories

My eyes open in a dark room
I sit up and look around
I'm in my bed, my soft comfy bed
I can't believe it, it was just a dream
But it seems so real.

Hannah Jones (13)
The Green School, Isleworth

Material Love

A love letter from the boy next door,
A dozen roses flung upon the floor.
Chocolates, flowers, an iPod full of songs,
Symbols of a romance that's been and gone.

A new bird's tune,
A bright new moon.
A peaceful, white dove,
A brand new love.

Two boys after just one girl,
Oh how love can be a whirl.
Yet the girl says 'No' to both,
Material gifts won't gain her troth.

Many think love's just a game,
But others know it's not that lame.
Because love can only be earned with love,
And not with a silly snow-white dove.

Love is precious, love is gold,
But love cannot be bought or sold.
Love must be shown and can't be taught,
Love that occupies every thought.

Caitlin Furborough (11)
The Green School, Isleworth

Playing Cards

Four families in one pack,
With rules they must abide,
The kings, queens and aces,
With jokers on the side,
The clubs, hearts, diamonds and spades,
Lay quietly on the pile,
While people shuffle, trade, fish and cheat them all the while,
But no one really understands that life in play is hard,
As no one really thinks about the life of a playing card.

Sarah Sayer (13)
The Green School, Isleworth

Have You Done Your Homework Yet?

'Have you done your homework yet?'
'Yes,' I smoothly lied,
When actually I hadn't,
This fact I had to hide.

It's a shame school gave us homework,
It really was a curse,
I always left it to the last minute,
That always made it worse.

My homework was always calling to me,
Always in the back of my mind,
Time for my homework,
I was reluctant to give and find.

So I always got bad grades in my homework,
I didn't stop to think,
'Will this affect me later in life?'
I never made the link.

And now I'm forty and living at home,
With my parents and one big regret,
I never truthfully answered the question,
'Have you done your homework yet?'

Elise Dowding (13)
The Green School, Isleworth

Snow!

Snowdrops are furballs, all white and soft,
They make a brilliant blanket,
It tastes like ice cream and smells so fresh,
It gives me a shock when it lands on my flesh.

Snow so white and cold,
Never stops even when told,
On it goes, swirls round and flows,
Wherever it wants, it goes.

Maryam Ellouis (13)
The Green School, Isleworth

Contrast

It's cold, dark and snowing,
The trees are bare and white,
No birds up high are singing,
Or feeling the warm sunlight.

I move towards a country,
In my mind's eye I see,
A sun that's golden yellow,
Glistening down on me.

I feel the warmth flow through me,
And through all the living things,
As sunshine spreads its tender wings,
And holds us in its rays.

But then I'm back again once more,
And see the ocean of snow,
And marvel at nature's contrast,
And life's eternal change.

I will feel the warmth again,
As I move from here to there,
But always to return,
To breathe this silent floating air.

Salma Yehia (11)
The Green School, Isleworth

Snow

Snow is white,
It's bitter but bright,
Cos it turns to ice,
When there's no light.

Snow is magical,
Very fanatical,
Makes people's loneliness change to happiness,
Cos snow is white.

Amirah Farook (12)
The Green School, Isleworth

Beauty . . .

What is it to be beautiful?
Is it for a blossoming daisy,
To be as pure as fallen snow
With a true golden heart
Or to be trampled and bruised?

Or is it for an elegant butterfly,
To be radiant with colour?
To glimmer with every flutter,
Or its paper-thin wings creased and torn,
Is this what we call beauty?

Or is it the early morning dew,
Glistening with the rays of early sun,
Coating everything in sight with a luminous glow?
Or its sticky substance seizing helpless prey,
Is this what beauty means?

Or is it indescribable,
Only known once it is seen or heard,
The definition altering to the object described,
Beauty, only we can detect,
This is what we call beauty.

Sarah Jane Norman (14)
The Green School, Isleworth

Snow

School should be shut
I don't like this cold hut

Snow is falling on the ground
I can't touch it, I'm not allowed

If I were at home
I would be outside playing and having fun
With all my friends

The fun will never *end!*

Lottie Richardson (12)
The Green School, Isleworth

Happy Seasons

Yellow roses
Paddling pool
New sunglasses, really cool
Dreaming in a splash of sun
Holidays have just begun

Blue Smarties
And friends forever
Curly locks and purple heather
Muddy wellies covered in grass
Childhoods don't have to pass

Red wrapping paper
Bright white snow
Twinkly lights which glitter and glow
Flying full tilt down a snow-covered hill
Stockings waiting on a window sill

Fresh green shoots
And skies so high
Sparrows singing as they fly
Scribbling a heart on the back of your hand
Running barefoot through the sand.

Maisy Allen (12)
The Green School, Isleworth

My Heart Drops Through My Chest

My heart drops through my chest
It's almost here, the time has come
That one true love who'll steal my heart
I dare not deny about my love
My eyes are blinded by this true beauty
I'm so struck, my face is numb
Who is he, is he the one?
That special one I dream of day by day
Is this not true love or am I blind?
My heart pumps out my chest just like a gun
We're stuck together, it's a strong love
When I look in his eyes I see my faith
I'm out of this world, I'm no more here
I'm in this place so far and near
Are you willing to test our love?
Nothing can make us depart
Is this love here to stay?
My heart drops through my chest
And he's holding it in the palm of his hands
He'll hold it tight and take much care
For he's the one, I dream of day by day.

Samira Thomas (14)
The Green School, Isleworth

Evermore

I walk through the flame,
I walk to the door,
Into the world of evermore.

The sky is green, the grass is blue,
Cows go quack and ducks go moo,
The river is not water but it is goo,
And the clocks when they chime shout, *'Boo.'*

The trees all talk, shout and whisper,
Animals sit around the table and eat dinner,
Turtles are worshipped and put on pillars,
The noises they make go *zinger, zinger, zinger.*

When the sun goes down,
The moon comes out,
No one makes a sound,
As the moon sings loud.

What a strange place this evermore,
So I walk through that first door,
Into the real world, such a bore,
Back into reality, for evermore.

Sahr Mian (14)
The Green School, Isleworth

Silent Passing

Conversation into light,
Through my dreams, ignite.
Receiving the penalty to pay
As you let yourself take away.

Dreamers wandering through deserted streets,
Another weary heart beats.
Piercing eyes snap in silence,
No sound to record, no image of violence.

Only my mind can regret things,
Snarl and annihilate.
Yet with love to help us through,
Take away hate before it's too late.

To turn to love, to speak with love,
Eyes wink of hope.
To no one is this easy, some a game to play
As yet love fades away.

Staring at broken faces, move over a few paces.
Is it best to stop or carry on?
Use our thoughts, silently passing.

Eloise Hemmings (13)
The Green School, Isleworth

Life

Life is full of surprises.
It can bring happiness.
It can bring traumas.
It can be neutral.
It can be and bring, well . . . anything.

Life is our friend.
Life is our enemy.
Life is unfair.
Life is a catastrophe.
Life is life!

Life is full of surprises.
It can bring happiness.
It can bring traumas.
It can be neutral.
It can be and bring, well . . . anything.

Life is a quest, waiting to be explored.
It can be funny.
It can be sad,
But it will be a shock.

Hodan Hassan (14)
The Green School, Isleworth

The Man From France

There was an old man from France
Who loved to sing and dance
He would practise all day
Until the sun got away
And the moon would come up to prance

Every day he did the same
All his friends thought he was lame
So just then
He taught Max and Gem
But then it became a game.

Molly Mills (11)
The Green School, Isleworth

My Fab Fisholly Friend

My fab fisholly friend
Will surf with me till the end
She's jollyostic and grey
She'll conker the sharks when they invade
I'll catch her lavish prey
Her smelliest and fishiest pride of the day.

Oh my fab fisholly friend
Halfway through the water's end
You're my Hawaiian board surfer
My 4 x 4 water glider
You're as graceful as a swan
And as beautiful as a butterfly.

Yes my fab fisholly friend
Our journey at the sunset of water's end
You're my fantastic funny companion
And the best friend I'll ever know
Although you live away from me
Deep down, I will never let you go.

What animal am I?

Makeeda Brown (13)
The Green School, Isleworth

One Night

One night I went in the woods
To find something
I wish I could
Something in the shadows
Like a snake hissing its name
Waiting for me to come
Calling me like a song

Searching but not seeing
Tree to tree
Losing my mind

The moon takes over
Now that daylight's behind
Looking for the shadow
The voice so mocking

Can't take much more
Breath by breath
Step by step
Till my death.

Hannah Alexander (13)
The Green School, Isleworth

Shattered Dreams

When I was younger I believed that dreams came true,
That everyone had and everyone pursued,
As I got older,
My dreams got bigger, wilder and much more imaginative,
On my 21st birthday, I went out to pursue this dream,
I had longed to come true.
I did everything I could,
Everything I had been taught,
But when I came back,
As well as my heart,
My dreams were shattered too.

Shaan Janjua (13)
The Green School, Isleworth

Emotions, Emotions

Anger is fire,
Once it's lit it grows higher.
It never stops,
It keeps on burning,
Is like a roller coaster,
It keeps on turning.

Love is roses,
Once they're planted they grow higher.
They twirl and twirl in the summer's wind,
But make sure you're aware of its thorns.

Jealousy is a monster,
Once it wakes it will bite.
Be careful, it will creep up unexpectedly,
And may take your life away,
But if you're careful and gentle
It will be asleep before you know it.

Emotions, emotions,
It's always their fault.

Miranda Lopez (13)
The Green School, Isleworth

The Thing

Did anyone want to be here?
Of course not.
Was anyone happy?
Of course not.
Had the Nazis taken over?
Yes.

As the night wind danced,
A chill filled the air.
Nothing could be chanced
While the victims were scared.

Two by two they entered the 'thing',
The machine that could kill,
The machine that was king,
The machine that would win.

As the taste of fear spread like a disease,
Death was around the corner.
Had the Nazis taken over?
Yes.

Mia Carruthers (12)
The Green School, Isleworth

Love

Love, love
If you have love
You'll have to move.

Love, love
What should I do?
Should I move or love?

Love, love
All it does is just fray,
If it doesn't fray, it will stay.

Love, love
But deep down he's there
If he's not, there's where?

Love, love
How can this stop?
If it won't stop, it will pop.

Love, love
What can we do?

Kajol Bhukhureea (13)
The Green School, Isleworth

Heaven

Heaven, Heaven, glorious with glee,
With angels roaming and singing free,
The sun shines brightly,
Ah its golden rays,
Birds sing a new song,
Ping, ping, pong.

I walk down its golden streets,
The weather's perfect, nothing out of place,
Flowers blooming from the sweet grass,
The smell of sour lemon hits you with a blast,
I lay back and dream about the day,
Dreaming about the day that I'll be back to stay.

Heaven, Heaven, it's the sweetest dream
With angels roaming and singing free,
Heaven's where no sorrows lurk,
With spirits leaping, bouncing, jumping,
Heaven, Heaven, what can I say,
Can I die now? It's the only way.

Iyinoluwa Oshinowo (13)
The Green School, Isleworth

In The Rain

I feel so complete
When I'm in the rain;
I feel no sorrow,
I feel no pain.
It may give me a cold,
But I don't care,
There's a calming sensation
From grass to air.
The feeling of love,
I don't have, I will gain,
Because my heart falls open
As I stand in the rain.

Renéa Cato-Green (13)
The Green School, Isleworth

Man On Moon

For hundreds of years, Man has wondered
How the moon came into being
Now it's destiny, to find the answers
But by only flying to Moon

Seconds to be on top of Moon
Wondering if all hard work will have paid off
No turning back, no changing the present
Mustn't give up, be brave, be brave

The moon itself shown to be lifeless
Though we spot the beauty of the darkness
Smiling at the camera as if so proud
Thinking if Man would be on TV

The flag on the moon with red and white stripes
Proves that Americans' dream has finally come true
Step by step leaving a gift behind
For hundreds of years work's paid off
Oh yes, Man is thrilled.

Zahra Rizwan (12)
The Green School, Isleworth

I Can't Seem To Sleep

I can't seem to sleep
Not a wink or a peep
Not a second or hour
I use all my power
Just tossing and turning
Some sleep I am yearning
Shadows I wake up to
Of hours I have few

I hate that beep, beep
That ruins my sleep
Every night I weep
Let me sleep, sleep, sleep.

Georgina Keok (12)
The Green School, Isleworth

Anger!

This emotion is the worst emotion you would ever want.
If you want this horrible beast to disappear it can't.
It's like a leech crawling up your whole body finding its next prey.

It controls your mind and takes your kind words into play.
It's a selfish feeling that you feel overcoming your heart.
I warn you now, but never forget that horrible creature that lurks around here,
It may come anywhere, maybe it's already here or there.

Don't show fear to it or it'll capture you within.
Your soul should be hiding from this beast or it would just disappear.
I would worry for anyone who hasn't heard or read this,
They may even be lucky to dodge this emotion.
This emotion is a dark, dreadful living thing
I can't even have the words cross my lips.

Its shadows cross its next prey when it's all alone.
If you catch a glimpse of this emotion,
I would give you this advice only, *run*!

Chloe Bevan (12)
The Green School, Isleworth

What Are The Feelings?

Walking down the street and there,
Driving past pair by pair
Are the traffic lights,
All so bright.
And by the ever changing lights are the people,
Love, friendship, hate they share.
Like the light I think,
Always changing, on the move,
Waiting, growing higher, moving down,
Always found in any town.
Never can anyone ignore,
The fact almost all adore the ever changing traffic lights.

Evelyn Hartnell (12)
The Green School, Isleworth

WWW

WWW dot
A few clicks from being whizzed away
Whizzed like a rocket shot
On the world wide web.

From place to place
Click here, click there
A wild cursor and mouse chase
On the world wide web.

A voyage through the skies above
Feel free to roam
The sites we all love
On the world wide web.

And then it happens and we're shaken free
As a parent shouts, 'Shut that thing down,
Stevie!'
And we slowly, so reluctantly leave
The world wide web.

Chika Chima (13)
The Green School, Isleworth

My Walrus

My boisterous yet colourful walrus
It's so hairy like a horse
With a scary, hairy face
My wishy washy wet walrus
Who is called Mary
My colourful swallow full walrus
My ugly, wugly, hugly walrus
Who smells of onion, it's a . . .
Squishy, squashy bunion which sounds like a monion
But he's my ugly colourful, hairy, scary Mary walrus
My very, very smelly welly walrus
I love you.

Rachel Aminat Rodipe (12)
The Green School, Isleworth

You Know It's Autumn

The leaves, golden brown
Crisp and strong scented
The acorns and conkers
Have that familiar smell
You know it's autumn.

The damp scent
The darkened sky
People in coats and scarves
You know it's autumn.

The fog and mist
People sitting by radiators
Grannies in their favourite chairs
You know it's autumn.

Warm soup and hot chocolate
Halloween is on its way
Pumpkins and sweets
You know it's autumn.

Zoe Watts (13)
The Green School, Isleworth

Goodnight My Sweet Lovely

His little eyes
His little nose
His little paws
His quivering body against my chest
His heart beating a million to a minute
His little whiskers tickling my face
But he suddenly stops twitching
As still as a stone he sat there
His heart slowing down
His little eyes began to close
Still no movement not even a twitch
No more gleaming eyes
No more twitching nose
No more quivering
And no more little heart beating a million to a minute
He was gone
Forever
Goodnight my sweet lovely.

Megan Delia Maingot (12)
The Green School, Isleworth

Love

Love is like a ray of sunshine,
A ray that's gold and so divine.
Love is like a dewdrop in spring,
A dewdrop of hope, which will sing.

Love can be a visit to Hell,
A visit with a vile smell.
Love can be a truth, so unfair,
A truth that no one wants to share.

To me, love is a dream come true,
A dream that makes me think of you.
To me, love is life's best mistake,
A risk that you and me should take.

Rosie Knox (14)
The Green School, Isleworth

Elephant And Castle

I've always wanted to visit Elephant and Castle,
I just never thought it would happen like this,
Hiding from the brave bombs,
Giving our loved ones their last kiss.

I didn't know what would await me,
In the place that would be like my saviour,
Help me, please help me,
No one would do me a favour.

By myself, lost and lonely,
With just the comforting breeze to be my friend,
But even that was swallowed up by people's presence,
My heart was broken, waiting for someone to mend.

Drawing what I knew would be my last breath,
I searched the space, the crowded, noisy space,
Looking for a flicker of hope, someone to run to, someone to love,
My eyes close, my lips turn dry, if only I had a familiar face.

Amy Grant (13)
The Green School, Isleworth

Race Is Life's Game

Separated by race,
Depends what you look like,
To where is your drinking place.

Too scared to complain,
Too scared to stand out,
Too scared to express what you're thinking about.

Sure they agree,
How could they not?
But then again, it's them against me.

They don't look alike but inside they're the same,
Like the old, the young,
Race is life's game.

Lily Mitchell (12)
The Green School, Isleworth

One Small Step Was All It Took

One small step was all it took
One small step which started it all
Like planting a seed into the future
A seed that would grow into a tree, strong and tall.

That day how the Earth looked up smiling
How remembered that day would be
That day when man walked on the moon
How we all lived so happily.

A stepping stone in the right direction
A day of success and joy
A day for everyone to feel proud of
A moment no one could destroy.

One small step was all it took
One small step which started it all
As so much work went into the moment
This achievement shall never fall.

Natalija Krivosic (12)
The Green School, Isleworth

Edward

Pale, white, granite-like skin,
His eyes as golden as the Queen's pure gold crown,
Bronze hair like an Olympic bronze medal.

His touch is so cold,
My teeth start to chatter.
His scent, so sweet,
You've just walked into a candy shop.
His sight, so truly mesmerising,
You can't take your eyes off him.
He is a drink of ice water on a hot day,
A drink which makes you forget all your worries.

How can this immortal be classed as an ordinary human?

Ayesha Saiyed (13)
The Green School, Isleworth

Love Can Make You Crazy

Trying to remember all he has done,
Trying to remember all the fun,
Sitting alone, all by myself
His picture is still on my shelf.

Trying to forget the way he died,
Trying to forget they way he tried,
Sitting alone, taking my pills,
Hoping that one way it kills.

Trying to destroy the feeling of a hook in my eye,
Trying to destroy the feeling to die,
Sitting alone in the dark,
The only noise is a dog's bark.

Trying to stay awake, until the morning break,
Trying to stay awake, remember that love's not fake,
Sitting alone, taking my pills,
Knowing that it kills.

Kareba-Savelle Kariuki (13)
The Green School, Isleworth

Empty

In my life I seem to find
The feeling bewilders me,
It overwhelms me,
A black cloud fills my mind.

Taking deep breaths, consoles me,
A fog of sorrow drifts by,
Nobody knows how I feel, I can't tell them
No matter how hard I try.

Depressed, alone, unforgiven,
Nothing compares, it's not forgotten,
Trying so hard no to drown,
Standing still as a mist drifts around.

April Marshall (12)
The Green School, Isleworth

Does Love Mean Anything?

Does love mean anything,
Or is it just nothing?
They always say, 'Listen to your heart,'
But how?

I look out in the street,
For someone I can meet,
But everyone passes me by,
I guess I'm too shy.

Are all of them taken,
And is there any left for me?
Love is all around,
But I did not succeed.

The wind howled to me,
And my hat soared away,
I will find it when I'm happy,
Which just isn't today.

Dallas Gadd (12)
The Green School, Isleworth

Fly High Little Bird

Fly high little bird away from this tree,
Now you have no need for me,
My nest is too small, for you and all.

Never come and call again,
For this is your end,
You know all you need,
So go, go little bird away from me.

Goodbye my darling,
Leave me singing,
Wipe your tears away,
For you cannot stay,
Fly high little bird.

Chloe Hudnott (14)
The Green School, Isleworth

Young Love

When I was 19
I went to a fantasy land
It's where I met Prince Charming
Who took me by the hand.

I didn't believe any of this
I couldn't believe it was happening
Until he fell to the ground
And pulled out a diamond ring.

The day had come
The bells were ringing
When we entered the church
Everyone was singing.

Now I'm happy
Because my dreams have come true
It's all because
I'm married to you.

Maira Abbasi (13)
The Green School, Isleworth

The Nature Season

The winter flowers flow to the ground like it was a river
but suddenly it rained, I got soaked.
But never be ashamed,
there is a house full of people where I can go to.

The summer love is upon us
and the nature season is with us
until the summer dies out
and doesn't come until next year.

The autumn has come with the leaves turning colour,
when I am in the autumn sun
I lie on the dry grass reading a book and lying on a towel
so my back does not get covered in grass.

Tricia Lane (13)
The Green School, Isleworth

Dream On

Smiling, surreptitiously, secretly.
Years of fakery, compiled into one.
Hiding our desires, too shy
To stand up for what we believe in.

But now we don't care what people say.
All we want to hear is the word, his word.
We fight for our rights like an army of love,
Here to stay, not going away.

A man of miracles, miracle man,
A man of miracles he was.
I'd love to be the angel in his dream,
The dream which saved the world.

The wind, paused for a breath,
The trees, stopped for a sigh of relief.
The world bowed down before him,
Martin Luther King.

Shivani Brooking (12)
The Green School, Isleworth

Hell

There's a place in the dark where the animals go,
You can take off your skin in the cannibal glow.
You can run with the daemons and play with the ghosts,
You can feast with a soul and the body it hosts.

You can swim in the hate of the pit of despair,
You can burn in the fire of Lucifer's lair.
As you creep through the dark over perilous lands,
Take the dagger and gather the blood on your hands.

You can run, you can scream, you can hide in a hole,
But the devil still rules you cos he owns your soul.
All that hurt that you gave, all the tears that were shed,
But you're here forever because you are dead.

Sophie Holland (13)
The Green School, Isleworth

Martin Luther King Jr

'I have a dream,' he said
'I have a dream that there will be no segregation
And we'd all come together, yes the whole nation
In love and unity.'

Then his manful mouth opened wide again
Like the opening of a cave
And shouted to the crowd
No one should be enslaved.

Then the lifeless microphone spoke again
'I have a dream that all hearts can bring
This is our chance, this is our chance
To let freedom begin.'

Now this man's dream has come true
We all now know what we should do
Be calm and peaceful, like the gentle seas
And live this day on in love and unity.

Rekayla Shanice Harriman (13)
The Green School, Isleworth

Blueberry

Little, little blueberry
Doesn't taste like raspberry
Dark and small and tastes so good
Different from the other food

Little, little blueberry
As sweet as a strawberry
Darker skin and smaller size
As small as our little eyes

Little, little blueberry
When I see you I'm happy
I love strawberries and raspberries
But best of all are blueberries.

Karen Mok (12)
The Green School, Isleworth

Am I Alone?

Steps fade away in the distance. I listen; intent to hear
They fade away like everything else, stripped me from my fear
And when they come back, the memories are near,
My one and only mother, her whisper I can hear

But she is gone, and no one to replace her
Now I am alone, my life an anxious stir
And those who were so close to me shone away in fear
Of having to look after me and tend to my good tear

So good tears I weep and look down
For the end is near, should I really frown?
One stripped of their guardians have no one in life
But they know that love is there in the afterlife

The plunging water looks up at me as I hold onto the end
I can hear her voice call me, shivers it sends
My life crushed, lonely, no one at home
And as I jump I think, am I alone?

Sarah Hadj-Lakchal (14)
The Green School, Isleworth

Love

I'll give you my love one day
When you say you love me when we're in the hay.
I wish you would just say it because I know you do,
Please oh please, just would you?

The meaning of love is sweet like flowers
And it blazes like a house on fire.
Once you love someone the fire will never dwell
It will live for evermore.

Love to me is like a rose
It grows day by day
So I hope you say it when we're in the hay . . .
Hopefully one day.

Scarlet Gilbart (12)
The Green School, Isleworth

Obama's Flag

'Yes we can,' he said.
'Make a change,' we said.

'I have a dream' was said.
'But dreams come true' was written.

As I climb my mountain of liberty
Whilst holding my floating flag, full of sympathy.
The flag sat down, just to mourn,
That it had lost all hope because of war.
It felt lost, lonely and all torn.

But now I've tried to sew it up,
As these lifeless hands reach out to me.
With their eyes full of hope
And their camera's flash, trying to be free.
Just like the fifty stars sitting on the flag,
With their hands spread out,
Empty.

Chenelle Olaiya (12)
The Green School, Isleworth

Love, Life And Music

Love is as blind as the eye of the beholder,
Love is as sweet as the day it was born.
Give love time to grow and be stronger,
But lock it in your heart to keep it warm.

Life is a question which needs answers,
Life is a puzzle that can't be solved.
Mess with life, mess with power,
Life is as safe as a mouse with a cat.

Music is as pure in the mind and soul,
Music is more beautiful than the sun.
Life without music is like life with injustice,
Listen to music, feel the love.

Seraphina Adebayo (14)
The Green School, Isleworth

The Girl Who Dreamt Of The Stars

She gazed at the sky, she glanced at the stars,
Wondering what there did lie.
From her eyes tears did fall, she did feel so small,
With the stars she wanted to fly.

The stars shone so bright, with brilliant light,
In the night so silent and dark.
She lay on the ground, not making a sound,
'She'll never get there,' sang the lark.

Deep breaths she took, she didn't dare to look,
Past the cliff she did standeth upon.
The breeze whipped her hair, at the sea she did stare,
And she thought of her life just begun.

Then jumpeth did she, straight into the sea,
But she knew she was flying so fast.
For her dreams had come true, her soul knew it too,
Now she could live with the stars.

Sophia Alison (13)
The Green School, Isleworth

The Flamingo Poem

I live in the zoo in Peru
And Pingo was his name-o
And I have a long neck
So I can reach the deck
I catch the fish
Cos that's my dish
I live in the zoo with my crew

I live in the zoo in Peru
And I am peach and that is true
I have wings to help me swing
I love to sing
With my friend Sabrina
Who is a ballerina
She is elegant, swelligant
Unlike an elephant
But she is a lovely friend to me.

Lucy Pearce (12)
The Green School, Isleworth

The Call

The rush of water
The sound in my ears
Of my family calling
I will go to them
They will come to me
We will stick together
Forever

As we go together
We are one
One mind, one body
Invincible
Against the current
We will stay together
Forever.

Jasmine Onstad (11)
The Green School, Isleworth

Cat

When darkness arrives
Cat is out in a trance
She is there when the moon
Greets the stars in the sky
Her emerald green eyes
Glint into the dark
Mice scatter in fright
At the sight of her dagger-like claws

Cat leaps on the flowers
And ruins the roses
She prances and dances
Scares a bird off her perch
Leaves a streak in the night
From her jet-black coat
Then dashes back in
Like she never went out.

Naomi Edwards (11)
The Green School, Isleworth

Mice

I think mice, are rather nice
Their tails are long
Their faces are small
They live in an old crummy hole
They dance at night
They sleep at day
And at dawn they scurry away
Their ears are pink
Their fur is grey
And their teeth are as white as the moonlight
They run about the house at night
And nibble things
Because they don't know what's wrong or right
But I think mice
Are rather nice.

Jemima Macken (14)
The Green School, Isleworth

Snow Poem

Snow is falling to the ground
And not making any sound.
Like a blanket that covers the town
It never makes me frown.

Snowflakes fall into my hair
Then melt into the air.
Children are playing and having fun
While their parents are eating a bun.

It starts to get late,
It's five past eight!
So we decide to go in
By accident I hit my shin.
And now I have a big bruise,
That was my snow news.

Elizabeth Allen (12)
The Matthew Arnold School, Staines

What Nonsense

'Mummy, Mummy, there are men on the moon with shovels,
saws and dynamite with cords!'

'What nonsense young girl! There's none on the moon,
the spacemen will tell you so.'

'But Mummy, don't you see, their ship's right there,
crammed full of all those men!'

'You speak only nonsense,
now go to bed and forget your silly ol' tale!'

'Mummy, oh Mummy, but don't you hear their grinders of granite
and crushers of chrome eating away at the moon?'

'You silly young girl, whatever next!
Are there monsters in your story too?'

'Of course there are, why don't you know?
They blast them with lasers and freeze and push them with beams
to destroy those beasts of rock!
But for the slugs of slime, they use these all the time!
A blasting sonic box!'

'Now you've gone too far little missy!
What could all this gain?'

'The crystals of energy is what it gains . . .'

Connor Hutnell (12)
The Matthew Arnold School, Staines

Friends Poem

F riends are forever
R eally someone you can trust
I think my friends are unique in their ways
E veryone has their ups and downs
N o one is ever left out
D on't worry the bad times are always pushed aside
S haring secrets with your best friends.

Nicole Bryce (12)
The Matthew Arnold School, Staines

Snow Poem

Snow is falling, swiftly, gently.
Each flake falls uniquely and differently.
Fresh snow begins to fall to the ground,
As my excitement doubles and my heart begins to pound.

School has been closed for the day
And the kids on my street shout, 'Hooray!'
I take a look at my swimming pool,
And it's turned into ice which is pretty cool!

Another thing that happened with the snowy scene,
It shimmers and covers like a blanket of dreams.
This is the first time ever I have seen snow
And now I wish that it would go!

It's been in magazines, on TV, in the news!
And my family cannot book their cruise!
The sea has frozen, it's not gone yet!
It won't melt for another week, I bet!

So now it's the end of my snowy day,
And now on a cold bench I lay.
For the snow has really brought me down,
It was fun at first, not so now!

Rebecca Belbin (12)
The Matthew Arnold School, Staines

Valentine's

Here comes Cupid with his bow and arrow,
Pierces my heart and many others,
For this special day I pray to give it to someone close.
I love you in the words of this day,
I hope to say it to a person someday,
With meaning, heart and passion.

Caitlin Hay (11)
The Matthew Arnold School, Staines

Sleepovers

Sleepovers are lots of fun,
Messing about and having fun.
Big bags of sweets that weigh tons,
Invite my friends that are the true ones.

Staying up late and having a joke,
We're all hyper from drinking Coke.
Sweets are all over the floor,
Some of the girls are starting to snore.

Pillow fight! Feathers everywhere,
Nail varnish goes flying, so do the bears.
The room's a tip,
If Mum sees the room she's going to flip.

Photos and videos we start to take,
Mum comes in and shouts, 'It's too late.'
We jump under the duvet but when Mum shuts that door,
We all jump out and play some more

It's starting to get light outside,
Run down the stairs, it's breakfast time.
Look out the window, it's snowing like mad,
'Can we go out Mum?' 'No not yet, too bad!'

Kirstie Walker (12)
The Matthew Arnold School, Staines

A Windy Night

It was a windy night,
A cat screeched,
A bin crashed,
Branches banged against the window,
It was a windy night.

Dogs bark,
Owls hoot,
Foxes run across gardens,
It was a windy night.

Mice scarper across the floor,
Birds' nest in the trees,
Moles tunnel deeper and deeper,
It was a windy night.

People stay indoors and drink hot drinks,
It was a windy night.

Joshua (12)
The Matthew Arnold School, Staines

Games

Games are made for fun
Games are made for entertainment
Games are made for learning
Games come in different types of genres
Games can kill boredom
A game could be adventure
A game could be action
A game could be fantasy
A game could be fighting
A game could be horror
Staring obliviously at the screen
Deeper and deeper as you get further into the game
Until you hear the phone or hear someone calling to you
And you leave the game paused, hoping to return soon.

Daniel Green (12)
The Matthew Arnold School, Staines

Friends Poem

They mess around and insult each other,
Tell each other secrets they don't have to cover.
Having a laugh that's what it's about,
We are weird that's no doubt.

We mess around and trash the room,
Mum thinks my room is a place of doom.
We have good times and pointless laughs,
Run to the shops down the paths.

These friends are the best, they are the ones,
They are like the sky to my sun.
The good times we do have so much,
I'm so glad we stay in touch.

Hannah Browne (11)
The Matthew Arnold School, Staines

There Was A Reindeer In My Wardrobe

There was a reindeer in my wardrobe Mum,
I heard it in the night.
And if you don't believe me Mum,
There's my top, it gave a bite.
Also the hole in the ceiling is a giant giveaway.
And the dent in the wardrobe (which is probably where it lay).

This final piece of evidence is one you can't deny,
One you can't laugh about or say it's a lie
See the reindeer came back Mum,
It was asleep on the floor
And now I'm going to tell you Mum,
It's hiding behind the door.

Ellie Daniels (12)
The Matthew Arnold School, Staines

Valentine's Day

14th of February is Valentine's Day,
My gift for my date
Will make him cheer, yay!

Love is a strong word,
Passionate and true,
When I get a chance
I'll say I love you.

Valentine's Day,
The most romantic day of the year,
Come on now,
Let's see you shed a romantic tear.

Lucy Wakelin (11)
The Matthew Arnold School, Staines

Friends

Friends are just the best, better than all the rest.
They make you laugh, they make you cry,
Maybe even poke your eye,
But you always know that they will be there,
They will always be there to care.

When you need a helping hand,
Wherever you turn, your friends will be there,
Always looking out for you, in every single way,
They always make my day.

No matter what you do,
Your friends will stick by you.

Stella Burke (11)
The Matthew Arnold School, Staines

Time

Time is quick, it flies right by
Time is ticking again and again
Time is a killer inside a bomb
Time is a countdown for a missile
Time can be a trigger waiting for your time to come.
Time is a signal, it howls when it hits twelve.
Time can be set forward and back
Time can be trouble if you miss the bus
Time can be mobile inside a little watch
Time is important, we all need it.

George Aldridge (11)
The Matthew Arnold School, Staines

Why Oh Why?

I sometimes wonder why people stop and stare
I really don't know why
When I speak they run away
I really don't know why.

Maybe it's because I'm a monster from Mars
But my mum told me I'm no different from the rest
So now I'd like to go to school
I wonder if I will get bullied
But I'll just scare them away.

Matthew Almeida (12)
The Matthew Arnold School, Staines

I Wish I Were . . .

I wish I were a racoon
And curled up to sleep like a furry cocoon,
To eat fruit, nuts and corn,
Not forgetting to grab
The occasional crab,
From the day I was born.

To be a gazelle,
Would be really swell,
To have mighty black horns,
That tower so high,
Right into the sky,
And to run like a storm.

Sleek and smooth dolphin,
Wearing a permanent grin,
Loved by everyone,
Swimming so silent,
Not at all violent,
Beautiful in the sun.

I wish I were a mouse,
In a small cosy house,
Scuttling everywhere,
Meeting new friends,
Taking odds and ends,
Sleeping in the cold winter air.

Molly Rees (11)
The Royal Ballet School, Richmond

Come Back To Me, Tommo

(Inspired by 'Private Peaceful' by Michael Morpurgo)

I do not sit alone and weep,
For I know you are under the same sky.
But are you warm, safe, fed or even dry?
Come back to me, Tommo.

Some nights, I sit and remember,
All the picnics by the river,
The gentle breeze made me all a-shiver.
Come back to me, Tommo.

I drown in my sorrows till morning light,
When day breaks through, all I see is you.
In my sleepy, drowsy head
What would you do?
Come back to me, Tommo.

Spring is here now,
And the birds are singing from above.
But where are you, my only love?
Come back to me, Tommo.

Rows and rows of cross upon cross,
Is one of them yours?
No, you are with the birds that fly.
My heart aches, but it's time to say goodbye.
You did not come back, Tommo.

Isabel Lubach (13)
The Royal Ballet School, Richmond

Colours
(in the style of 'Christina Rossetti')

What is green?
Green is mean, vile and cruel just like a ghoul.
What is yellow?
Yellow is light, nice and bright and full of might.
What is red?
Red is bed comfy and soft, not too aloft.
What is blue?
Blue is no clue, for the unanswerable answers
Like why do cows moo?
What is purple?
Purple is alert, always on the watch,
Making sure you've got the plot.
What is white?
White is lonely, it's the only crayon not used in the box.
What is pink?
Pink is a wink, when you've done well it's sure to dwell.
What is orange?
Orange is confused, it's usually never used in a poem.
What is black?
Black's on your back, cute and shy, but not in the night sky.

Daniel Myers (12)
The Royal Ballet School, Richmond

A Happy Ending

I stumbled across the footpath,
As the scary noises scream,
My eyes are shut tight
Not knowing what is behind me.

Shadows lurk in the darkness,
The night drew over my head,
It's a small dark alleyway
With noises coming from everywhere.

Little light shines at the start,
Not where I am now,
Things scurry across the floor
As I move further along.

What's going to happen next?

There's a light at the end of the darkness
I thought it would never come,
My happiness is taking over me
I am free!

Lewis Charlton (11)
The Royal Ballet School, Richmond

Power

The great obsession that comes from power
Increases higher in every hour
Until the final path is set
With sorrow and infinite regret

And when the final time has come
The beating of the shining sun
Upon the rioting kingdom arise
Anger burning in their eyes.

And when the nightfall doth begin
The anger and hatred once within
Has come at last to a silent sleep
And a calmness, oh so deep.

So when the power you receive
Overpowers all who believe
Use it well and use it wise
As the opposition could bring surprise!

Ashley Hardwick (12)
The Royal Ballet School, Richmond

The Mysterious Tunnel

What leads beyond the tunnel?
No one knows,
Behind the heaps and heaps of snow,
The web-like branches, concealing the start
And nothingness inside it,
It is so very dark!

I feel the iciness inside of me,
Tightening my muscles and extracting my heat,
The terror, the dread, the obscurity,
It can be anything you want it to be!

Is it a friend, or is it a foe?
If we don't commence, we shall never know,
So now we edge, into the gloom,
To await our destiny, to await our doom!

Caleb Pinkham (12)
The Royal Ballet School, Richmond

Daddy, Wake Up

I loved my dad, well most people do
Just those little things like tying up my shoe
We would always play games and run around
We'd play hide-and-seek but I would always be found
He really was close to my heart
He pricked me inside like pricking your thumb with a dart

It wasn't until that dreadful day
When unfortunately he passed away
I said, 'Daddy wake up,' but it was just too late
I can't believe that I was only eight
Of course, of me he is a part
And he is still alive inside of my heart
That is where he will be forever and longer
My bond with my father could not have been stronger.

Augustus Payne (12)
The Royal Ballet School, Richmond

It's My Turn Today

I heard them again,
One by one getting slain,
Each one of them connected to me,
Their voices - short of glee,
Two days ago we were full of cheers,
But now all I could see were tears,
I knew it - it's my turn today,
Much to my dismay,

I could feel a constant beat in my head,
Never letting go - as someone once said,
My heart was pounding at a terrific speed,
I always felt it was something to heed,
I convinced myself that they were dreams,
But now it doesn't look like how it seems,

They say life flashes before you,
I must say - it is true,
I'm falling to the ground,
No sound . . .

It's my turn today.

Aathirai Gnanasampanthan (12)
The Tiffin Girls' School, Kingston-upon-Thames

The Driver And The Youth

When will it come, the people sigh, weary and resigned;
Time and vehicles pass them by with other things in mind.

And, lacking any sense of haste, it finally approaches.
He regards us with distaste, as if we are cockroaches.

His hostile eyes, they glare at us; we watch him cruelly smile.
Once the driver stops his bus, he waits for quite a while,

Then finally opens up the doors and lets us all come in;
While he sneers, juts out his jaw and scratches at his chin.

It seems the driver likes to make us feel intimidation -
Oh, the pleasures he can take from Oyster confiscation!

A frail old lady gets on last, and gives a shaky flinch
As he slams the doors shut fast - they miss her by an inch.

Next stop there stands a youth alone, and as the bus draws near,
We catch a glint of his headphone, protruding from his ear.

As soon as that lone youth gets on, there is a steady stream
Of blaring music coming from his pestilent machine.

He drops an empty can of Coke, his jeans reveal his bum,
His strong deodorant makes us choke, he spits out chewing gum.

He shouts, he swears, he makes phone calls, with no respect for us.
He draws graffiti on the walls; he thinks he owns the bus.

A sudden jolt, the lights go dim, the driver's on the stair;
He spots the youth, and orders him to promptly go elsewhere.

The youth looks up, their gazes meet, it's stalemate in a flash;
Prejudice and pride compete, arrogances clash.

They engage in silent warring, minutes pass us by.
So intense and yet so boring, neither blinks an eye.

One by one, we start to rise, and leave the stubborn pair.
To me, it would be no surprise if they're still standing there.

An eye is for an eye, they claim. A tooth is for a tooth.
Both are equally to blame: the driver and the youth.

Louis Norris (13)
Tiffin School, Kingston-upon-Thames

Remembering A Promise

Laughing, flying, spinning, swimming through the summer sky
Summer light thinning, morning running from the night
Escaping from the promises that hold us in our time
Will you remember me now when summer comes again to shine?

Now the leaves are falling faster, summer's at an end
Happily ever after, try again to mend
Deep beneath the surface broken glass is creeping in
As you stare into the morning light remember me again

Flying, dying, chasing fleeting shadows from the sun
Falling ever faster now, the battle never won
Together through the summer skies we're burning down as one
We'll wish we could do something more together as we run

Remembering a promise as you took me by the hand
You led me through the shining lights, a distant magic land
You lit me up under the stars together as we lay
A bed of clouds, a golden gate, remember me one day.

James Ireland (15)
Tiffin School, Kingston-upon-Thames

Granny On The Loose

For today is the day
That I was meant to pay
My dear old granny a visit.

She was stuck in her fridge
In the middle of the bridge
A chav walked past and said, 'Is it!'

It started to rain
And she was left in pain
As the door had been frozen shut.

A dog strolled past
And peed on it
What a dirty little mutt!

Jenna Buller (14)
Tolworth Girls' School, Surbiton

So The Story Goes . . .

If you look inside a girl's heart
You'll see how much she really cries.
Things are hidden,
Best friends and lies.
Only when she goes to sleep
Will the pain go away
But when she awakes
She hates the new day,
Behind the make-up, behind the hair
There's a tag saying
Handle with care
She's feeling so sad, so insecure,
Not like those haters,
Not fake, she's pure.
She's feeling despair,
Good seeds have been unsown,
Those haters are waste chicks
And she's in a waste-free zone.
She needs to escape,
Escape from herself.
She wants to run away.
This isn't good for her health.
She should have let it go,
Walked away with nothing more,
Her life is now over,
She's now at death's door,
But she will always be with us,
Just up in the sky.
I never once thought,
This is how she would die,
As we stand there in church
Praying for our mate,
Those haters say they're sorry,
But they know it's too late.
As she's lowered into her grave,
We sadly say goodbye
How we'll miss our loved one
But there's no more tears to cry.

Tia Crocker (16)
Tolworth Girls' School, Surbiton

Teddy

A teddy bear all alone
Like a dog without a bone
A teddy bear all alone

No one to hug, no one to hold
No secrets left to be told
No one to hug, no one to hold

Left behind
Nowhere to find
Just left behind

No blanket to cover
When the wind makes you shudder
No blanket to cover

Everyone gone
But not for long
Everyone gone

Back tomorrow
No more sorrow
Back tomorrow

Back from holiday
Back today
Back from holiday

A hug and a kiss
I was sorely missed
A hug and a kiss

Tucked up in bed
With my owner, Fred
Tucked up in bed

Not left behind
Easy to find
Not left behind.

Georgia Conlin (13)
Tolworth Girls' School, Surbiton

World In Darkness

A beautiful world
Happiness all around
The blue sky, the green forest
But we knew that this world
Is going to end one day

It was a balmy evening, September 2012
Bad news was spread
Everywhere I go all I could hear
That the world is going to melt down!

No food, no water
People were dying of hunger
No phone, no TV or radio
Scientists were trying to save the world

People were running away
Changing countries to countries
But when your death is after you
You can't run anywhere from it.

People, scientists had lost their hope
Then there was nothing to do
All the lights went off
Where you see the darkness
So that was it
The world ended in the darkness.

Amna Shahzadi (13)
Tolworth Girls' School, Surbiton

My Little Brother

My little brother is so sweet,
To hear the pitter-patter of his feet,
His favourite food is chips and fish,
He likes it in his special dish,
I love him loads, he loves me,
We are a very big happy family!

Jamie Beckett (14)
Tolworth Girls' School, Surbiton

Bad Dog

I'm ever so sorry
I ate your brolly
I know there's rain outside

I slept on your face
And the cat I did chase
All around the inside

Your slippers I chewed
Now your feet are in the nude
I slobbered on your toes

You put on your shirt
Just to find dirt
I'd brought in through the windows

I hid your shoe
Put it in the loo
You had to wear sneakers to work

Chasing your car
But not for far
I was caught by Uncle Kirk

He put me on a log
And shouted, '*Bad dog*'
I went home and peed on the sofa.

Alice Jones (14)
Tolworth Girls' School, Surbiton

Blah, Blah, Blah

These poems we're reading,
They're not what they seem.
Teachers find a deeper meaning
Than what the poet wanted it to mean.
They get ripped apart until the fun is gone.
I can't find anything that rhymes with 'gone',
So this is the end of the poem.

Chloe Painter (15)
Tolworth Girls' School, Surbiton

My Wonderful Cat

She's playful, funny and cute,
She puts the telly on mute,
She's black, fluffy and cuddly,
And guess what she is to me . . .
The best cat in my life.

She sleeps in the conservatory,
Her midnight stroll is short,
Her steps are soft and slow,
Then she sleeps, sleeps, sleeps,
Till the morning comes.

When morning comes she miaows for food,
I give her the tasty meaty food,
She sits on the window ledge,
To see all the schoolgirls go by
And waits for me to come home.

I come home from school
And as the evening comes,
I give her a cuddle,
While she sits on my lap,
Then off I go to bed.

I love my cat. My cat loves me!

Hannah Price (12)
Tolworth Girls' School, Surbiton

Identity

I 've lost my identity
D on't know who I am anymore
E veryone speaks a different tongue to me
N o one understands what I'm saying
T rying to fit in with everyone else
I 've given up
T rying to be what
Y ou expect me to.

Holly Williams (16)
Tolworth Girls' School, Surbiton

Things Are Different

In the 60s everything was different
The clothes, culture and attitudes to proclaim
Groovy, colourful, bright and unusual
Safe, friendly, nobody to blame
Free, cosy, know each other's name
And then things change.

In the 90s everything was different
The clothes, culture and attitudes to proclaim
Plain, glittery, whatever you want
Careful, ambience, lively
Success, freewill, say what you think
And then things change.

In the 21st Century everything was different
The clothes, culture and attitudes to proclaim
Rebellious, loud, difference, tight
Impact, scared, crime, everybody to blame
Lost, threatening, *bang!*
Things have changed.

From what we used to be
Guns, crime and other goings on
Have rearranged to the times that are now gone.

Emily Gear (16)
Tolworth Girls' School, Surbiton

Another Day

One day has gone
Another one is here,
The same old stuff
Will never disappear.
All the rows
Fights and fuss
Has all gone for nothing
The day I lost her trust.

Hannah Dandridge (15)
Tolworth Girls' School, Surbiton

Waiting

Silent, still waiting
Wind rushing through the sunburnt grass
Waiting, waiting

Heart beating, blood flowing
Waiting, waiting

Victim, close.
Stalker, unseen,
Waiting, waiting.

Paws, press on dry solid mud
Waiting, waiting
Claws ready
Waiting, waiting

Pounce!
Tiger, elegant, vicious
Victim, innocent
Tiger, full, no longer hungry

No more waiting
No more waiting
No more waiting
No more waiting.

Chantelle Lenaghan (12)
Tolworth Girls' School, Surbiton

My Friend Molly

My name is Bobby,
My friends are being gobby,
Their names are Molly and Polly.

Molly is playing with her dolly,
Polly keeps telling me to be jolly,
But how can I when I'm in love with Molly?

Phoebe Hardy (13)
Tolworth Girls' School, Surbiton

Le Me Be Remembered . . .

To lie in a field
and look at the sky.
I never once thought,
this was how I would die.

This day's been short,
for so many of us,
thousands have died
but what's all the fuss?

Before it's all over
there'll be a few million more,
those lovely young people
killed in this war.

The sound of the guns
are fading away,
I can feel my life ending.
In God I must pray.

Don't leave me to rot
or I will be lost,
let me be remembered
in a place with a cross.

Aimee Nicol (16)
Tolworth Girls' School, Surbiton

Babies

Babies are so fun and cute,
They make you laugh
And make you go up and down
Like a plotted graph.
But when it comes for them to cry
They cry so hard they just make you
Want to hug and squeeze them,
But that's not all, there's so much more.
Babies are so incredible.

Zaynab Malik (12)
Tolworth Girls' School, Surbiton

The Beach

A dazzling blue sky
Not a cloud in sight
With a gentle sea breeze
Not enough to fly a kite

Soft sand underfoot
It goes on for miles, golden and gleaming
The sight is amazing
You believe you're dreaming

Small, foamy waves
Bubbly and bright
Lap gently against the shore
Warmed by the midday heat

Though the beach is sparkling
All chirpy and cheery
When sunset comes
It becomes dark and eerie

The light fades away
And the little waves grow
Washing away the events of the day
Preparing for a fresh start tomorrow.

Grace Royal (12)
Tolworth Girls' School, Surbiton

Diamonds

Romantic red diamonds
Glittering in the night
Like glistening pearls of the night
They're glamorous, sparkly and pretty too
But way too expensive for me or you.

Shannon Grinsell (14)
Tolworth Girls' School, Surbiton

A Day At The Zoo

A day at the zoo,
What a brilliant idea.
We can go see the lions,
As they scare us with fear,
Or perhaps the monkeys
As they swing tree to tree,
Actually I don't mind the chameleons
As they change colour so easily,
Or how about the penguins
As they waddle side to side,
Or we can go see the giraffes
And see their necks which are so high,
Maybe we could feed the elephants
As they stomp around the place,
Or we could swim with the dolphins
And give them a race,
Or go see the frogs
As they jump in the air,
And then the snakes as they slither everywhere.
A day at the zoo is so much fun,
Lots of things to do for everyone.

Leanna Nejad (12)
Tolworth Girls' School, Surbiton

Bringing Up A Single Parent

It's hard bringing up a single parent,
They always want, want and want,
They always want to stay up late,
Or bring home some really strange friends.

You have to let them wake you up,
So you can get ready for school,
You have to let them brush your hair,
And brush down your clothes.

It's tiring sometimes,
The way you always have to please them,
You have to let them fret over you,
As otherwise they will get terribly worried.

It's hard bringing up a single parent,
They always need all your attention,
You can't take your eye off them for a minute,
As they could be doing anything.

However, I love my mum very much,
So bringing her up is my very own choice.

Jessica Leech (14)
Tolworth Girls' School, Surbiton

Emotional Duel

Like a boiling pot bubbling up
Overflowing, filling you up,
It's too much, it's about to burst!
It's the thirst,
For coming out and exploding, showing your worst.
Then here it comes . . . it's overtaken,
Happiness beyond belief; and if I am not mistaken
My face has lit up and a smile started to grow.
This joy that has built up is about to blow,
That's it . . . it's out, for the whole world to see
Now I will never forget that joy is the key.

Lauren Fox (13)
Tolworth Girls' School, Surbiton

Nowhere But Everywhere

I look and see nowhere but everywhere,
The silky sand I once tread upon,
The milky sapphire sea,
The snow white birds
And all that lies beside me.

I listen to nothing but everything,
The whispering gentle breeze,
The crashing and churning of the sea,
The heart of the bird cawing
And the palm trees swaying beside me.

I feel like I'm elsewhere,
Singing in the sunset,
Laughing with the other children,
Oh so joyfully.

But that time has ended,
That was there and then,
I'm here and now - all alone,
Once more I look to see nowhere but everywhere.

Tooba Tahir (12)
Tolworth Girls' School, Surbiton

I'm Going To Be A Bridesmaid

Not long now, only seven weeks to go,
until I stand beside my sisters - three in a row.
I'm going to be a bridesmaid for Mum and my step-dad,
and the intensity of the wait is going to drive me mad!
We've been extremely busy choosing flowers, frocks and frills
and then there is the worry of how we pay the bills.
I'm very, very excited and I'm very, very proud,
I'm going to be a princess and stand out in the crowd.
Some dainty shoes, a pretty dress and a tiara too
to look my very best when Mum and Richard say, 'I do!'

Paige Fayers (13)
Tolworth Girls' School, Surbiton

Do You Remember?

Our friendship was unique
You were like my sister,
We were that close.
Sure we had our ups and downs
But we always got through it.
We had been through so much together;
Laughter, heartaches, families and love.
You were always there for me
And I hope you can say the same about me.
I wonder where you are now
And if you remember our memories.

Remember the boom box on the school field,
And fun bus journeys before and after school.
Making new friends and being loud; good times.
I remember going to Thorpe Park
And going on Nemesis . . . 'Wahey!'
I wonder where you are now
And if you remember our memories.

Hannah Lyons (16)
Tolworth Girls' School, Surbiton

My Life! My Life!

I have no name, I am not the same.
I don't play any games,
Because I think I'm lame!
My friend is scary, he thinks he's a fairy.
He hates to be a Larry,
And his name is Gary.
Mum has no honey, but she has money.
She hates bunnies and thinks she's funny.
Dad hates to say
He owns 20 pieces of hay.
He chooses to stay,
Because he wants to play.

Afia Mannan (14)
Tolworth Girls' School, Surbiton

Michael Jackson

Labelled a legend, king of pop.
Started off in Jackson Five,
His music and passion
Will always be alive.

'Man in the Mirror',
A song with a meaning.
The lyrics so powerful;
The song full with feeling.

His death brought to many,
Sorrow and sadness.
Though today we think,
A lost legend is madness.

The voice was born,
The voice has gone.
From that voice,
We shall never hear another song.

Amy Hornsby (12)
Tolworth Girls' School, Surbiton

A Winter's End

As the last seconds tick away
Of this snowy winter's day,
The world tucked in,
Under a blanket of snow.

Only I know,
Who leaves the small footprints
Under the rose.

As the world drifts off
Into a deep sleep,
The silent owl calls.
Goodnight!

Jemima Davis (14)
Tolworth Girls' School, Surbiton

The Boy Around Four

If you were in their position, you'd care a whole lot more.
Walking the streets at night you'd find a boy around four.
His eyes are swollen, feet dragging behind.
Walking empty-handed, and with nothing to find.
If you question him slyly, you'll find no reply
'Cause this time he left without saying goodbye.
Clothes all ragged and feet so bare.
His tiny mind overloading, wanting someone to care.
His passion for love is way beyond his age,
Wishing in his life, he could turn the next page.
So I'll leave you with one thought of the young boy
Around four . . . next time you hear him crying,
Talk to him, he'd like that more.
The night I watched the young boy walking,
Was the last I ever saw,
I'm guessing nobody helped him,
I found his bloody shirt hung on his door.

Jennifer Culham (13)
Tolworth Girls' School, Surbiton

If Only

If only I could feel the touch of your hand,
The softness of your kiss,
The warmth of your hug.

If only I could tell you how much I love you,
How much I miss you,
How much I wish you were here.

If only I could have one more day
To tell you you're amazing,
That I need you
And I'm sorry that I couldn't,
I wouldn't.

Vanessa Hodge (15)
Tolworth Girls' School, Surbiton

Lonely Heart

All alone, sitting and thinking of what we used to be
I thought my life would be incomplete if there was no you and me
The tears I cry are not for you,
It's because I know I shouldn't, but I truly miss you
I thought that you and me were forever,
I guess that was another lie,
Love is a confusion, love is a game, I say I love you
But you don't say the same,
You say one thing and mean another,
You left me alone without saying a mutter,
And now I have a lonely heart,
I thought that we would never part
But now I'm left with a broken heart.
Finally I realise it wasn't meant to be
Now I realise you never loved me,
There was never going to be a you and me.

Natasha Beckett-Smith (13)
Tolworth Girls' School, Surbiton

Somewhere

The waves crash against the rocks,
The boats rocking near the docks,
The sun shines in the deep blue sky,
Upon the milky sand where I lie!

Seagulls caw above the sea,
I stand up, someone looking at me,
The wind whistling against my skin,
A pair of fins emerge very dim!

I plunge into the deep blue ocean,
Tumbling further down and down . . .
Away from town, away from city,
The bright red sun setting while I drown.

I'm going . . . gone.

Hafsah Rana (12)
Tolworth Girls' School, Surbiton

Love And Flowers

Love and flowers go together
It has been like that forever
Love is like a flower
You should watch it by the hour
If you want to keep it alive
Water will make it survive
You can give it away
Or you can make it stay
Either way you live day by day
If you don't try
The flower will die
And your life might fall apart
Eventually you'll end up with . . .
A broken heart.

Elizabeth De Goede (13)
Tolworth Girls' School, Surbiton

A Sonnet Of Mortal Embrace

Romeo: If I diss you with my dirtier hand
Your amazing figure has tempted me,
My lips, two blushing melons ready stand
To smooth rough edge of love, you devil-she

Juliet: Good fellow, you are worthy for my love
Which your forward behaviour shows in this
For even me, I am not from above
But mortal beings can embrace in kiss

Romeo: Can women and men not use their lips too?

Juliet: Yeah good lad, lips they must use to express

Romeo: OK, cannot bodies do what lips do?
I plead to your love may I have access?

Juliet: I don't express myself through my body

Romeo: Then merely think of it as a hobby.

Natasha Ivan (13)
Wallington High School for Girls, Wallington

In Doubt

On the day of the Haiti earthquake,
My homeland began to shake,
Residents drowned in the lake.

Above me there was rubble,
I knew that this meant trouble,
I want to curl up in a bubble.

Will I die?
Can I cry?
Will I die?

How I want to scream,
Am I living in a dream?
My tears begin to stream.

I shout,
Left in doubt,
What was this all about?

I need help,
So I yelp,
I need help!

Was my mother hit?
I'll find her in a bit.
Hold on that's it!

God wanted the earthquake,
He made the ground shake,
Caused people to die in the lake.

Please donate
It's not too late
Please donate.

Winnie Healy (12)
Wallington High School for Girls, Wallington

Man's Best Friend

They began as wild wolves, large and scary,
Massive sharp teeth and ever so hairy.
Their long hooked claws ready to grab,
Not one small ounce of fat or flab.
Their big bodies, muscular and strong,
Enough power to bring down King Kong.
People got scared and hunted them down,
Carried their dead bodies into town.
Now we are surrounded, but no one cares,
And we don't go and hunt them in their lairs.
Because they are cute, cuddly pets,
Wanted and loved, showing no threats.
Because a wolf may live in your house,
Maybe just catching the occasional mouse.
The wolf is a dog, so gentle and calm,
Surely they could cause no harm.
But it is true, this is a dog's history,
Their great ancestors are not a mystery.
But since becoming dogs, they have changed,
The motives in their mind have rearranged.
For the bond with a dog can be so strong,
With the right person a dog can really belong.
The only friend you can truly confide in,
If there is a secret you can't hold within.
And a dog will listen, and understand.
And if they could they would hold your hand.
It is said that a dog is a man's best friend.
And that saying is not a silly myth.

Natalie Arscott (12)
Wallington High School for Girls, Wallington

Stray Cat

I am a stray cat you see,
Being hit with a broom is not nice,
Always scrounging from bin to bin,
Only finding edible food once or twice.

The cold night air chills my skin,
The hairs stand up on my back,
Oh what I'd give to be in,
With a nice warm drying rack.

'Watch out there's that cat!' they shout,
Apparently I'm infested with fleas,
'He shouldn't be left to wander about,'
Oh give me a chance please . . . please?

People jump to conclusions,
Don't judge before you meet,
Sometimes they may be illusions,
'I'm fine, I'm on four feet!'

My owners left me when I was young,
How cruel . . . mean . . . unfair,
I suppose what's done is done,
I suppose they don't give a care.

Standing in the cold night air,
The stars twinkling above,
It's a shame my owners don't care,
Oh why, oh why don't I have somebody to love?

Sophie Herrington (12)
Wallington High School for Girls, Wallington

Fear The Night

A crackle of lightning
A rumble of thunder
Like a ferocious beast clawing at the blanket of darkness
But a breeze pipes up and sweeps it away

The flick of a light switch
A husky snore
Toes curled up in the warmth of a duvet
Street lights blinking and flickering out

The moon like a ghostly galleon
Sailing across the velvet sky
Flashing stars like the glint of a diamond
The rustle of leaves in a silent street

A road like an eerie lit ribbon
Curving and dipping through the darkness
A towering shadow stretched over the gravel
A tremble of fear and a piercing scream

The screech of a toddler
Similar to a cat's yowl
Lurking in the shadows preparing to pounce
Slinking silently in a streak of moonlight

A glitter on the horizon
A fiery, golden gift
A flock of birds singing the melody of morning
But the terror of the night is sure to return.

Rachel Barham (11)
Wallington High School for Girls, Wallington

Stop

I don't want you to leave me
I couldn't bear to see you go
I don't know why you just can't stop
But if you left, I'd want you to know

I loved you since the day I was born
The moment I could breathe
I am the luckiest girl in the world
Because you are the mother of me

Please don't die and leave me
If you did I couldn't cope
You helped me through the good and bad
So please Mum please don't smoke

I know you've already started
But this doesn't have to be your fate
Please don't smoke anymore
It really isn't too late

But I know it is
Please stop Mum
Please
Just stop
Please
Stop.

Sophie Garrod (12)
Wallington High School for Girls, Wallington

Summer Dreams

Summer, a lovely season!
The hot blazing sun, shooting straight at you!
Shorts, tank vests and skirts in different colours,
Ice creams to chill you out,
Everyone wearing sunglasses,
People putting suncream on,
Long, bushy, green grass full of people,
Picnics in the parks,
But what's best - summer holidays,
Summer - my favourite season!

Summer, not always great,
Sunburns for everyone,
Burning all your skin cells,
The sun making you sweat,
Too hot to run a marathon,
Sometimes too hot to go outside,
The forecast's showing heatwaves,
People getting frustrated because of the heat,
Summer, not always great,
But there's always the summer holidays!

Pooja Sunildath (12)
Wallington High School for Girls, Wallington

Fire

The fire shimmers then rages,
It burns on for ages and ages.

It causes terror wherever it may spread,
Lots of oxygen the flame is fed.

Everywhere around is destroyed,
It's what everyone's trying to avoid.

I am completely terrified,
Of this scolding, blinding light.

Mairisa Spiers (12)
Wallington High School for Girls, Wallington

Save Them

The ocean is a big long stretch,
Of silver, blue and white.
With coral reefs and rainbow fish
Dancing through the night.

Children playing on the beach,
Running away from waves,
While cameras flash and tourists smile
Seeing the legendary caves.

But then again, life's not always a ride,
The rainbow fish are forced to run and hide.
And do you know why? It's not cos of some shark,
Not cos of some big fish having a lark,
No, it's because of the human race.
Always up for a big long chase.
The real monster is the fishing boat.
The more their nets are full, the more they gloat.
We hear them laugh, cheer and shout,
Please stop, the fish are dying out.

Nicole Jashapara (12)
Wallington High School for Girls, Wallington

My Brother

My little brother Bobby
Has a favourite hobby
Making chaos and mess
With always more not less
He loves to play with his toys
Just like other little boys
He goes nuts in the middle of dinner
But he's not a very good winner
I think he is quite plucky
But I am very lucky
To have my little Bobby
And his favourite hobby.

Lindsay Farquhar (11)
Wallington High School for Girls, Wallington

I Am A Poem

I am a poem
Not a song
I can rhyme
Or tell a story

I am a poem
With verses or stanzas
I may have rhyming couplets
Or no rhyme at all

I am a poem
So take me as I am
Or I'll be out to get you
With an axe in one hand
So watch out!

Jessica Read (12)
Wallington High School for Girls, Wallington

Sky Taps

They're fluffy
They're puffy
They're wet and stuffy

They're graceful
They're hateful
They always rain on me

There are some
That come
In a frightful shade of grey

They soar
They pour
Like taps in the sky.

Ellie Clarke (13)
Wallington High School for Girls, Wallington

Springtime Morning

The wind floats across the field,
Gentle and slow, meek and mild,
The grass tips lift and sway with the breeze,
A perfect carpet of glinting green.

Spring brings a glint of what is to come,
Plants bask in the fresh new sun,
Daffodils turn yellow, faces towards
The orange of the morning glow.

The gentle warmth spreads all around,
Nothing can be heard, not a sound.

Kate McLaughlin (13)
Wallington High School for Girls, Wallington

Young Writers Information

We hope you have enjoyed reading this book - and that you will continue to enjoy it in the coming years.

If you like reading and writing poetry drop us a line, or give us a call, and we'll send you a free information pack.

Alternatively if you would like to order further copies of this book or any of our other titles, then please give us a call or log onto our website at www.youngwriters.co.uk.

Young Writers Information
Remus House
Coltsfoot Drive
Peterborough
PE2 9JX
(01733) 890066